Math Expressions

Volume 1

Developed by
The Children's Math Worlds Research Project

PROJECT DIRECTOR AND AUTHOR
Dr. Karen C. Fuson

This material is based upon work supported by the
National Science Foundation
under Grant Numbers
ESI-9816320, REC-9806020, and RED-935373.

Any opinions, findings, and conclusions, or recommendations expressed in this material
are those of the author and do not necessarily reflect the views of the National Science Foundation.

HOUGHTON MIFFLIN HARCOURT

Teacher Reviewers

Special Thanks

Special thanks to the many teachers, students, parents, principals, writers, researchers, and work-study students who participated in the Children's Math Worlds Research Project over the years.

Credits

Cover art: © Kerstin Layer/Age Fotostock

Illustrative art: Robin Boyer/Deborah Wolfe, LTD; Dave Clegg, Geoff Smith, Ron Mahoney, Tim Johnson
Technical art: Nesbitt Graphics, Inc.
Photos: Nesbitt Graphics, Inc.; Page 93 © C Squared Studios/Photodisc/Getty Images; Page 455 © Nick Green/Jupiter Images

VOLUME 1 CONTENTS

Dear Family,

Your child is learning math in an innovative program called *Math Expressions.* This program interweaves abstract mathematical concepts with everyday experiences of children. This approach helps children to understand math better.

In *Math Expressions* your child will learn math and have fun by:

- working with objects and making drawings of math situations
- working with other students and sharing problem-solving strategies with them
- writing and solving problems and connecting math to daily life
- helping classmates learn

Your child will have math homework almost every day. He or she needs a Homework Helper. The helper may be anyone — you, an older brother or sister (or other family member), a neighbor, or a friend.

Please decide who the main Homework Helper will be and ask your child to tell the teacher tomorrow.

Make a specific time for homework and provide your child with a quiet place to work. Encourage your child to talk about what he or she is doing in math class. If your child is having problems with math, please talk to me to see how you might help.

To make the concepts clearer, the *Math Expressions* program uses some special methods and activities. Two are described on the back of this letter.

Thank you. You are vital to your child's learning.

Sincerely,
Your child's teacher

continued ▶

- **Place Value Drawings:** Students learn to represent numbers with drawings that show how many hundreds, tens, and ones are in the numbers. Hundreds are represented by boxes. Tens are represented by vertical line segments. Ones are represented by small circles. The drawings are also used to help students understand regrouping in addition and subtraction. Here is a place value drawing for the number 178.

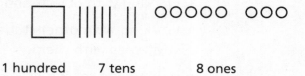

1 hundred   7 tens   8 ones

The 7 ten sticks and 8 circles are grouped in 5s so you can see the quantities easily and avoid errors.

- **Secret Code Cards:** Secret Code Cards are a set of cards for hundreds, tens, and ones. Students learn about place value by assembling the cards to show two- and three-digit numbers. Here is how the number 148 would be assembled.

Hundreds card   Tens card   Ones card   Assembled cards

Make Place Value Drawings

Estimada familia:

Su niño está aprendiendo matemáticas por medio de un programa innovador llamado *Math Expressions*. Este programa relaciona conceptos matemáticos abstractos con la experiencia diaria de los niños. Esto ayuda a los niños a entender mejor las matemáticas.

Con *Math Expressions* su niño aprenderá matemáticas y se divertirá mientras:

- trabaja con objetos y hace dibujos de problemas matemáticos
- trabaja con otros estudiantes y comparte con ellos estrategias para resolver problemas
- escribe y resuelve problemas, y relaciona las matemáticas con su vida diaria
- ayuda a sus compañeros a aprender.

Su niño tendrá tarea de matemáticas casi todos los días. Le hará falta una persona que le ayude con la tarea. Esa persona puede ser usted, un hermano mayor (u otro familiar), un vecino o un amigo.

Por favor, decida quién será el ayudante principal y dígale a su niño que se lo informe al maestro mañana.

Establezca una hora para hacer la tarea y ofrezca a su niño un lugar tranquilo donde trabajar. Anime a su niño a comentar lo qué está aprendiendo en la clase de matemáticas. Si su niño tiene problemas con las matemáticas, por favor comuníquese conmigo para ver cómo puede ayudarlo.

Para presentar los conceptos de manera más clara, el programa *Math Expressions* usa métodos y actividades especiales. Dos de ellos se describen en el reverso de esta carta.

Gracias. Su ayuda es muy importante en el aprendizaje de su niño.

Atentamente,
El maestro de su niño

continúa ▶

- **Dibujos de valor posicional:** Los estudiantes aprenden a representar números por medio de dibujos que muestran cuántas centenas, decenas y unidades contienen. Las centenas están representadas con casillas, las decenas con segmentos de recta verticales y las unidades con círculos pequeños. Los dibujos también se usan para ayudar a los estudiantes a que comprendan cómo se reagrupa en la suma y en la resta. Éste es un dibujo de valor posicional para el número 178.

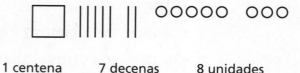

1 centena   7 decenas   8 unidades

Los palitos de decenas y los círculos se agrupan en grupos de 5 para que puedan ver las cantidades más fácilmente y eviten errores.

- **Tarjetas de código secreto:** Las tarjetas de código secreto son un conjunto de tarjetas con centenas, decenas y unidades. Los estudiantes aprenden acerca del valor posicional organizando las tarjetas de manera que muestren números de dos y de tres dígitos. Así es como se puede armar el número 148.

Tarjeta   Tarjeta   Tarjeta   Tarjetas organizadas
de centenas   de decenas   de unidades

Make Place Value Drawings

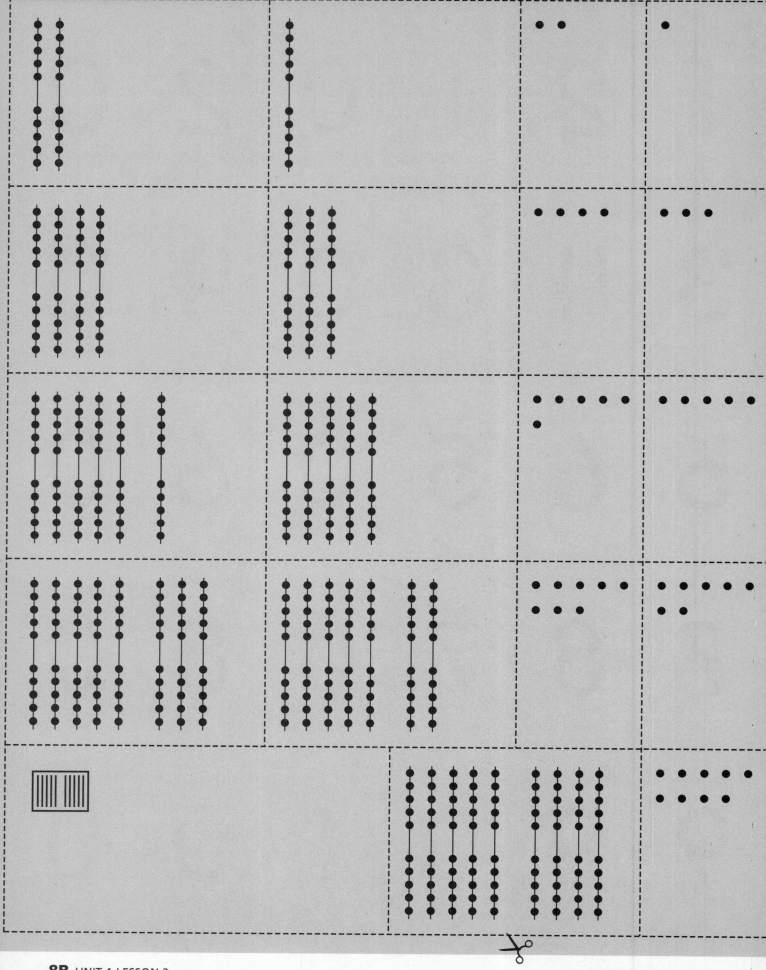

Secret Code Cards 1–100

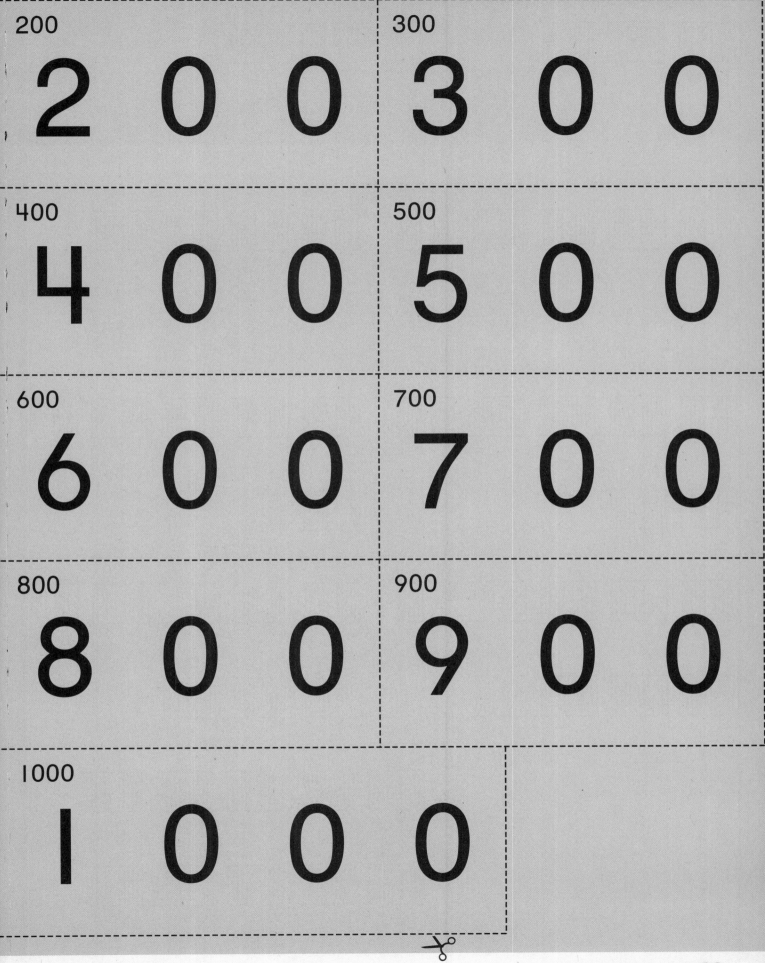

200
2 0 0

300
3 0 0

400
4 0 0

500
5 0 0

600
6 0 0

700
7 0 0

800
8 0 0

900
9 0 0

1000
1 0 0 0

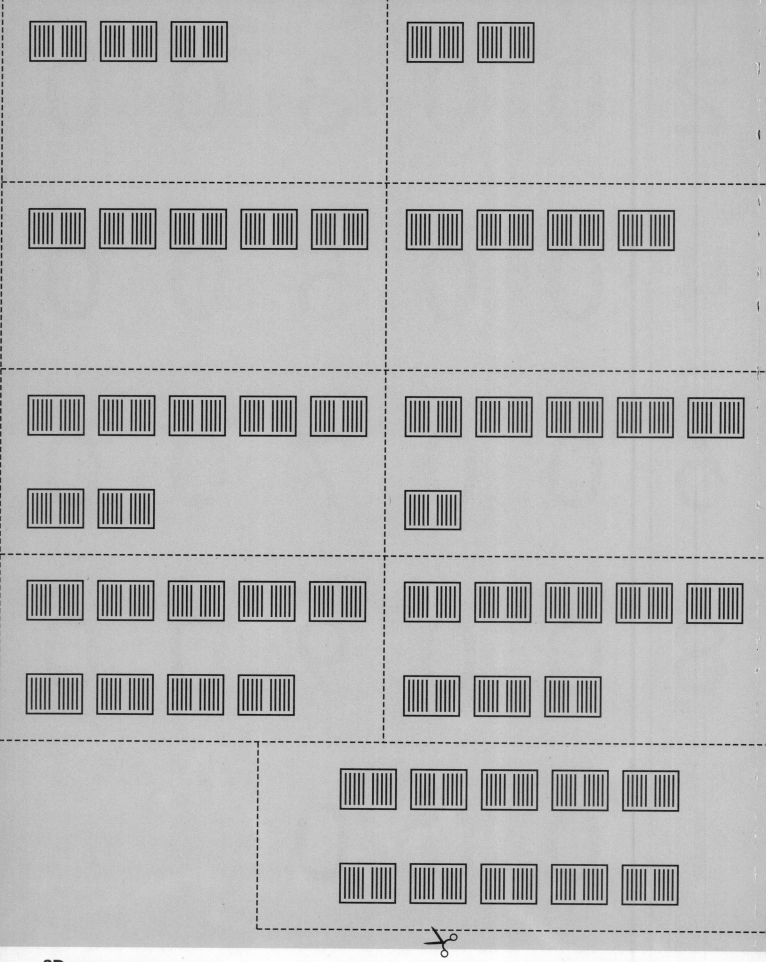

Dear Family,

Your child is currently participating in math activities that help him or her to understand addition and subtraction of 2- and 3-digit numbers.

Addition Methods: Students may use the common U.S. method, referred to as the New Groups Above Method, as well as two alternative methods. In the New Groups Below Method, students add from right to left and write the new ten and new hundred on the line. In the Show All Totals method, students add in either direction, write partial sums and then add the partial sums to get the total. Students also use proof drawings to demonstrate grouping 10 ones to make a new ten and grouping 10 tens to make a new hundred.

The New Groups Below Method shows the teen number 13 better than does the New Groups Above Method, where the 1 and 3 are separated. Also, addition is easier in New Groups Below, where you add the 2 numbers you see and just add 1.

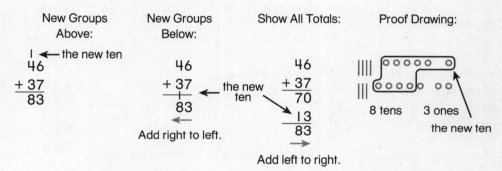

Subtraction Methods: Students may use the common U.S. method in which the subtraction is done right to left, with the ungrouping done before each column is subtracted. They also learn an alternative method in which all the ungrouping is done *before* the subtracting. If they do all the ungrouping first, students can subtract either from left to right or from right to left.

The Ungroup First Method helps students avoid the common error of subtracting a smaller top number from a larger bottom number.

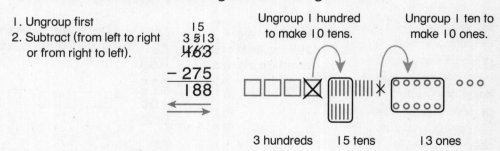

Please call if you have any questions or comments.

Thank you.

Sincerely,
Your child's teacher

Estimada familia:

En estos momentos, su niño está participando en actividades matemáticas que le ayudan a comprender la suma y la resta de números de 2 y de 3 dígitos.

Métodos de suma: Los estudiantes pueden usar el método común de los EE. UU., conocido como método de grupos nuevos arriba, y dos métodos alternativos. En el método de grupos nuevos abajo, los estudiantes suman de derecha a izquierda y escriben la nueva decena y la nueva centena en el renglón. En el método de mostrar todos los totales, los estudiantes suman en cualquier dirección, escriben sumas parciales y luego las suman para obtener el total. Los estudiantes también usan dibujos de prueba para demostrar cómo se agrupan 10 unidades para hacer una nueva decena, y 10 decenas para hacer una nueva centena.

El método de Grupos nuevos abajo muestra el número 13 mejor que el método de Grupos nuevos arriba en el que se separan los números 1 y 3. Además, es más fácil sumar con Grupos nuevos abajo, donde se suma los dos números que se ven y simplemente se añade 1.

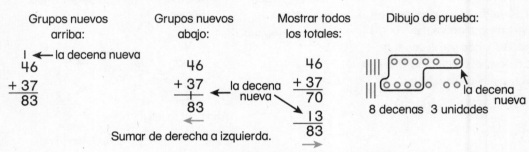

Métodos de resta: Los estudiantes pueden usar el método común de los EE. UU., en el cual la resta se hace de derecha a izquierda, desagrupando antes de restar cada columna. También aprenden un método alternativo en el que desagrupan todo *antes* de restar. Si los estudiantes desagrupan todo primero, pueden restar de izquierda a derecha o de derecha a izquierda.

El método de Desagrupar primero ayuda a los estudiantes a evitar el error común de restar un número pequeño de arriba a un número más grande de abajo.

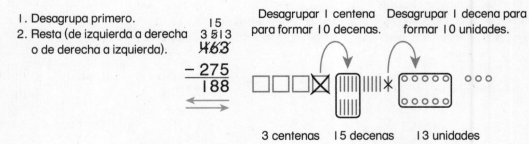

Si tiene alguna pregunta o comentario, por favor comuníquese conmigo. Gracias.

Atentamente,
El maestro de su niño

Explore Multi-Digit Addition

Lunchtime Diner

Sandwiches
Grilled Cheese $2.39
Tuna $2.57
Chicken $3.84

Sides
Veggies $0.74
Salad $0.98
Fruit $0.66

Drinks
Iced Tea $1.12
Lemonade $1.09
Bottled Water $0.99

▶ **Solve and Discuss**

Use the menu above to solve. Use a MathBoard or a separate sheet of paper to show your work.

1. Mr. Jackson ordered a grilled cheese sandwich and an iced tea. How much did his order cost?

_____

2. Mrs. Lin ordered a glass of lemonade and a chicken sandwich. How much did she spend?

_____

3. **Choose a Method** Kurt and Ana ordered two salads. Think of a fast way to find the total cost. Describe your method.

_____

_____

4. **Number Sense** Anne-Marie has only $1.50. Which two items could she buy?

_____

Going Further

► **Use the Guess and Check Strategy**

Use the pictures above to solve.

1. José bought two items. He paid with a $5 bill and two $1 bills, and got $0.50 change. Which items did he buy?

_____

_____

2. Explain how you found your answer.

_____

_____

_____

_____

_____

The Grouping Concept in Addition

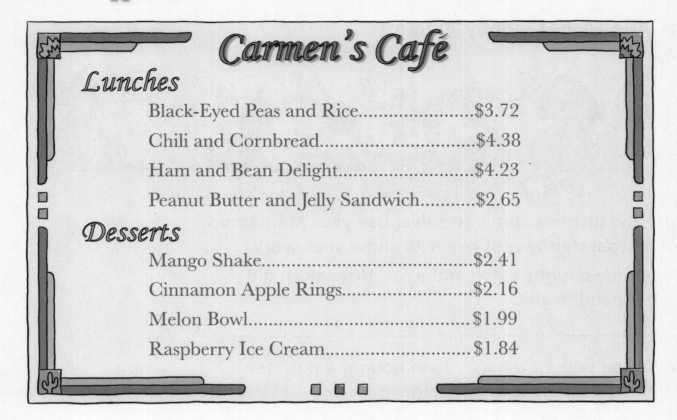

Carmen's Café

Lunches

Black-Eyed Peas and Rice.......................$3.72

Chili and Cornbread..............................$4.38

Ham and Bean Delight..........................$4.23

Peanut Butter and Jelly Sandwich...........$2.65

Desserts

Mango Shake...$2.41

Cinnamon Apple Rings..........................$2.16

Melon Bowl...$1.99

Raspberry Ice Cream.............................$1.84

▶ Solve and Discuss

You and your partner can take turns being a customer and a server at Carmen's Café. Follow these steps:

- The **customer** chooses two items from the menu.

- The **server** writes down the names and prices of the two items and figures out the total cost.

- The **customer** checks to make sure the total is correct.

Show your work on your paper.

Going Further

Name _____ **Date** _____

▶ **Add Larger Money Amounts**

Use the pictures above to solve. Use your MathBoard or a separate sheet of paper to show your work.

1. Jeremy bought a dog and a cat. How much did he spend in all?

_____

2. Keisha bought a horse. Juan bought a pig. How much did they spend together?

_____

3. Chan bought a cat, a duck, and a horse. What was the total cost?

_____

4. **Choose a Method** Rani wants to buy two rabbits. Think of a fast way to find the total cost. Describe your method.

_____

_____

5. **Number Sense** Betty has $20.00. Is that enough money for her to buy a cow and a horse? Explain why or why not.

_____

_____

Practice Addition

Going Further

Vocabulary

method
calculator
mental math

▶ **Choose Mental Math, Pencil and Paper, or Calculator**

Add or subtract. Then write what computation method you used. Write (p) for paper-and-pencil, (c) for calculator, or (m) for mental math.

1. $8.00
   − 7.50

   Method: _____

2. 79
   + 87

   Method: _____

3. 537
   − 91

   Method: _____

4. 495
   + 938

   Method: _____

5. $9.25
   − 4.01

   Method: _____

6. 2,000
   + 5,700

   Method: _____

7. $9,743
   − 5,221

   Method: _____

8. 12,534
   + 29,798

   Method: _____

9. $23,000
   − 14,000

   Method: _____

Solve each problem. Write whether you used paper-and-pencil, a calculator, or mental math.

10. Liz scores 20,000 points in her first turn. She scores 19,000 points on her second turn. How many points did she score altogether?

_____

11. There were 17,948 people at the basketball game on Friday night. There were 16,777 people at the game on Saturday night. How many more people were there on Friday night than on Saturday night?

_____

⟹ 12. **On the Back** Play the *Method Show-Down* game.

▶ Method Show-Down Game

Work in groups of three. Write the following methods on three separate index cards.

| paper and pencil | mental math | calculator |

To play the game.

1. Each student writes an addition or subtraction exercise using numbers up to 5 digits on an index card. Put the cards in a paper bag.

2. One student mixes the three method cards and distributes them to the group, while another student picks an exercise card from the paper bag. Each student then uses the method on his or her card to solve the problem. The first student to get the correct answer scores 1 point. Mental math may be really difficult for problems with large numbers.

3. Mix the method cards and repeat the activity. The first student to earn 5 points wins the game.

Practice Addition and Subtraction

Class Activity

Name _____ **Date** _____

► **Math and Literature**

Step 1: Make two spinners.

There are 46 stamps in a collection. There are 23 model cars in a collection. How many more stamps than model cars are there?

Step 2: Write names of collections on pieces of paper and put in a bag.

Step 3: Spin Spinner A twice to write a 2 or 3-digit number. Spin Spinner B twice to write a 2 or 3-digit number. Draw 1 or 2 collection names out of the bag.

Step 4: Use the numbers and collection names to write a word problem.

Act out the problems by modeling them on the MathBoard or with base ten blocks.

1. Write and solve a word problem using the rules above.

_____

_____

_____

2. Sarah has 143 buttons. How many more buttons does she need to have 199 buttons?

_____

3. Math Journal Write and solve more word problems about collections using the rules above.

_____

Class Activity

► Rock, Paper, Scissors

Rock, Paper, Scissors is a game. The players show a rock, paper, or scissors with their hands.

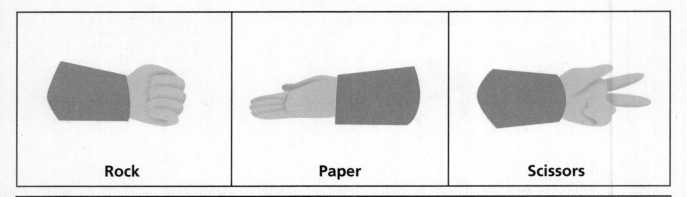

| **Rock** | **Paper** | **Scissors** |

Game Rules

1. The players throw their hand at the same time to show rock, paper, or scissors.

2. Rock crushes scissors and wins.

3. Scissors cuts paper and wins.

4. Paper covers rock and wins.

5. The player who scores a win gets 1 point.

6. If two players make the same throw with their hand, they must throw again.

7. The player with the most points wins.

4. List all of the different possibilities for one round if 2 players play the game?

5. How many different possibilities are there?

6. Play the game 10 times with a partner. Keep track of your results in a table.

Class Activity

► Measure Line Segments

Vocabulary

line segment
centimeter

Measure each line segment to the nearest centimeter.

1. _____

_____ cm

2.

_____ cm

3.

_____ cm

4. _____

_____ cm

5. _____

_____ cm

6.

_____ cm

Class Activity

Vocabulary
horizontal
vertical

▶ Draw Line Segments of Given Lengths

Draw each line segment.

7. a **horizontal** line segment about 7 cm long

8. a **vertical** line segment about 4 cm long

9. a slanted line segment about 13 cm long

10. a vertical line segment that is a little more than 2 cm long

11. a horizontal line segment that is a little less than 9 cm long

Vocabulary
perimeter

► Measure the Perimeter of a Triangle

Find the perimeter **of each triangle to the nearest centimeter.**

12.

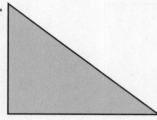

_____

13.

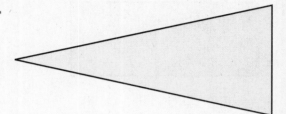

_____

14.

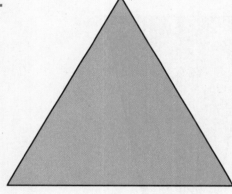

_____

15.

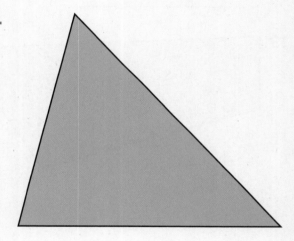

_____

16. Join the points to make a triangle. Find its perimeter.

●

●   ●

_____

► **Measure the Perimeter of a Quadrilateral**

Find the perimeter of each quadrilateral to the nearest centimeter.

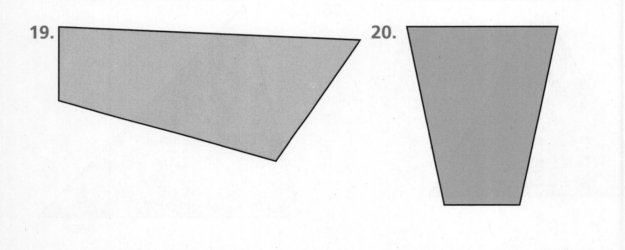

17. _____

18. _____

19. _____

20. _____

21. Join the points to make a rectangle. Find its perimeter.

● ● ● ●

● ● ● ●

_____

Dear Family,

Your child will be learning about geometry during this school year. This first unit is about the geometric figures called quadrilaterals. These get their name because they have four (*quad-*) sides (*-lateral*).

Students will learn about four different kinds of quadrilaterals in this unit.

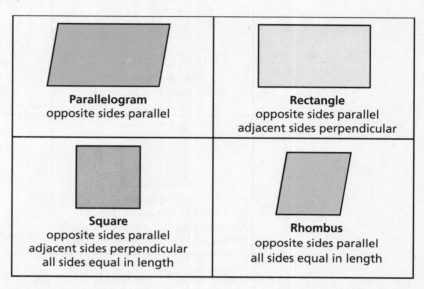

Parallelogram
opposite sides parallel

Rectangle
opposite sides parallel
adjacent sides perpendicular

Square
opposite sides parallel
adjacent sides perpendicular
all sides equal in length

Rhombus
opposite sides parallel
all sides equal in length

Each side of a quadrilateral is a part or a segment of a straight line. Your student will practice making careful measurements of line segments.

Students will measure line segments in centimeters in this unit. Centimeters are a convenient size for measuring and they are closely linked to the base 10 numeration system we use.

Your student will be able to recognize and describe different quadrilaterals by their sides. Some sides may be of equal length. Some sides may be parallel: they do not meet no matter how far they are extended. Some sides may be perpendicular: where they meet is like the corner of a square.

If you have any questions, please call or write to me.
Thank you.

Sincerely,
Your child's teacher

Estimada familia:

Durante este año escolar, su niño aprenderá geometría. La primera unidad se ocupa de figuras geométricas llamadas cuadriláteros. Éstas se llaman así porque tienen cuatro lados.

En esta unidad los estudiantes aprenderán acerca de cuatro tipos diferentes de cuadriláteros.

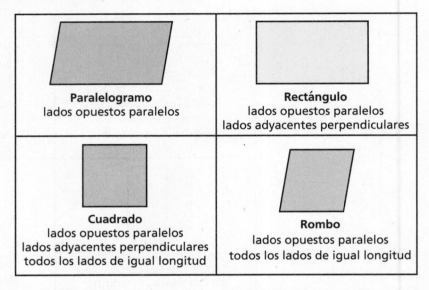

Paralelogramo
lados opuestos paralelos

Rectángulo
lados opuestos paralelos
lados adyacentes perpendiculares

Cuadrado
lados opuestos paralelos
lados adyacentes perpendiculares
todos los lados de igual longitud

Rombo
lados opuestos paralelos
todos los lados de igual longitud

Cada lado de un cuadrilátero es parte de un segmento de recta. Su niño practicará cómo medir segmentos de recta cuidadosamente.

En esta unidad los estudiantes medirán segmentos de recta en centímetros. Los centímetros son una medida apropiada y están directamente relacionados con el sistema numérico de base 10 que usamos.

Su niño podrá reconocer y describir diferentes cuadriláteros según sus lados. Algunos lados pueden tener la misma longitud. Algunos lados pueden ser paralelos: nunca se encuentran a pesar de lo largos que sean. Algunos lados pueden ser perpendiculares: cuando se encuentran, forman lo que podría ser el vértice de un cuadrado.

Si tiene alguna pregunta o comentario, por favor comuníquese conmigo. Gracias.

Atentamente,
El maestro de su niño

Measure Line Segments and Perimeters of Figures

▶ Define Lines and Line Segments

Vocabulary

line
line segment
endpoint

A **line** is a straight path that goes on forever in both directions. When we draw a line, we put arrows on the ends to show that it goes on and on. Here are some lines.

A **line segment** is part of a line. It has two ends, which are called **endpoints**. Here are some line segments.

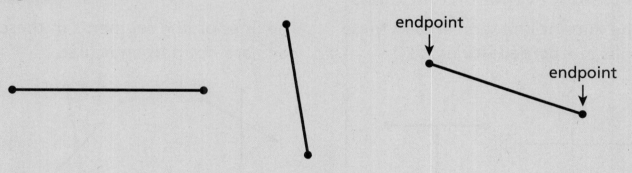

1. You can measure to find the length of a line segment, but you cannot measure to find the length of a line. Explain why.

_____

_____

_____

_____

Vocabulary
parallel
perpendicular

▶ Define Parallel Lines

The lines or line segments in these pairs are **parallel**.

The lines or line segments in these pairs are not parallel.

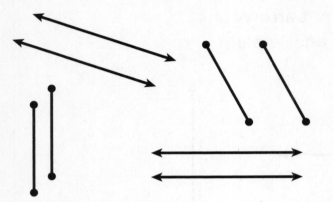
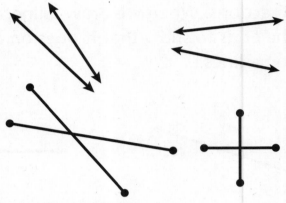

2. What do you think it means for two lines to be parallel?

_____

_____

▶ Define Perpendicular Lines

The lines or line segments in these pairs are **perpendicular**.

The lines or line segments in these pairs are not perpendicular.

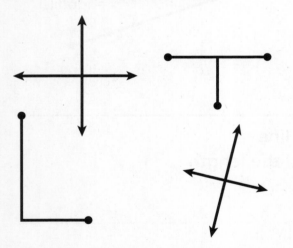
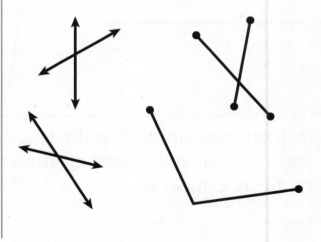

3. What do you think it means for two lines to be perpendicular?

_____

_____

▶ Identify Opposite and Adjacent Sides

Vocabulary
adjacent
opposite

Look at these quadrilaterals.

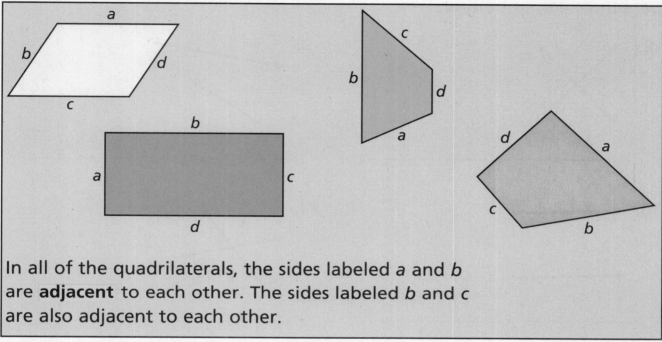

In all of the quadrilaterals, the sides labeled *a* and *b* are **adjacent** to each other. The sides labeled *b* and *c* are also adjacent to each other.

4. What do you think it means for two sides to be adjacent?

_____

_____

5. Which other sides are adjacent to each other?

_____

In all of the quadrilaterals, the sides labeled *a* and *c* are **opposite** each other.

6. What do you think it means for two sides to be opposite each other?

_____

_____

7. Which other sides are opposite each other?

_____

Class Activity

▶ **Identify Types of Lines**

Tell whether each pair of lines is parallel, perpendicular, or neither.

8.

_____

9.

_____

10.

_____

11.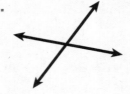

_____

12. Draw a pair of parallel line segments.

13. First, draw a line segment 3 cm long. Then, draw a line segment 6 cm long that looks perpendicular to your first line segment.

14. Name two perpendicular adjacent sides in this figure.

_____

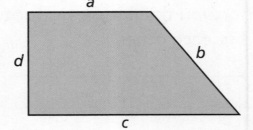

15. Name two parallel opposite sides in the figure.

_____

Class Activity

Vocabulary
parallelogram
quadrilateral

▶ Define a Parallelogram

All of these figures are **parallelograms**.

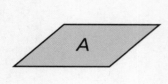 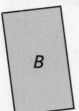 

These figures are not parallelograms.

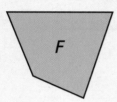 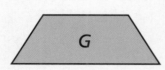  

Complete the sentence.

1. A parallelogram is a **quadrilateral** with _____

_____

▶ Measure Parallelograms

For each parallelogram, measure the sides and label them with their lengths. Then, find the perimeter.

 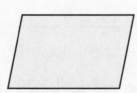 

2. _____ cm   3. _____ cm   4. _____ cm

5. Look at the lengths of the sides. What patterns do you notice? _____

_____

_____

Name _____ Date _____

Vocabulary
rectangle
square
rhombus

▶ Define a Rectangle

All of these figures are **rectangles**.

Adel said, "Rectangles are special kinds of parallelograms."

Complete the sentence.

6. A rectangle is a parallelogram with _____

_____

▶ Explore Squares and Rhombuses

These figures are **squares**.   These figures are **rhombuses**.

Takeshi said, "Squares are special kinds of rectangles."

Cora said, "Rhombuses are special kinds of parallelograms."

Complete each sentence.

7. A square is a rectangle with _____

_____

8. A rhombus is a parallelogram with _____

_____

Class Activity

Vocabulary
rectangle
square

► Find the Perimeters of Rectangles and Squares

Find the perimeter of each figure in centimeters *without* measuring all four sides.

These figures are **rectangles**.

9. _____ cm

10. _____ cm

These figures are **squares**.

11. _____ cm

12. _____ cm

13. **Write About It** How are rectangles and squares the same? How are they different?

_____

_____

_____

_____

_____

Class Activity

quadrilateral
parallelogram
rectangle
square

► **Describe Quadrilaterals**

Use as many words below as possible to describe each figure.

quadrilateral	parallelogram	rectangle	square

14.

_____

_____

_____

_____

15.

_____

_____

_____

_____

_____

16.

_____

_____

_____

_____

17.

_____

_____

_____

_____

Parallelograms, Rectangles, Squares, and Rhombuses

► Tangram Figures

Carefully cut out each figure along the dotted lines.
Make sure you cut as carefully and straight as you can.

Use your figures to create the patterns on Student
Activity Book page 63.

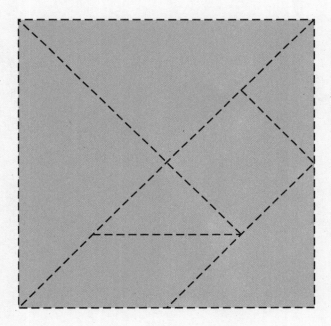

Going Further

Use your tangram figures from page 58A to make this cat. When you finish, draw lines to show how you placed the figures.

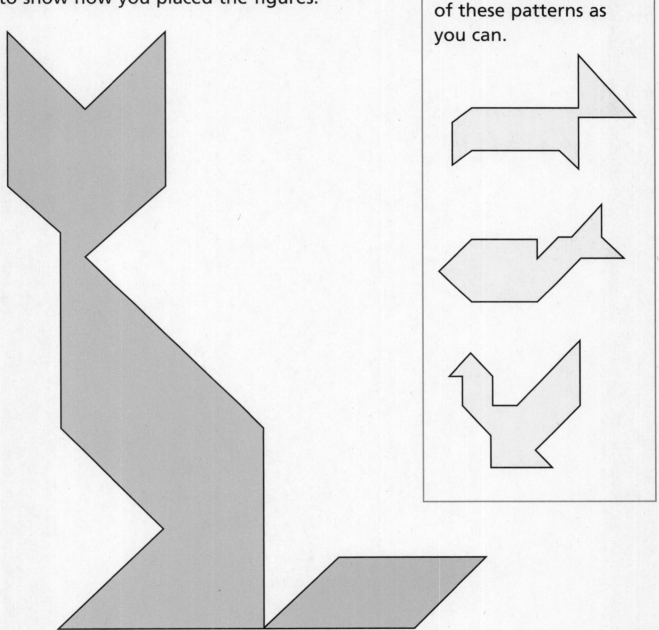

Try to create as many of these patterns as you can.

🔵 **On the Back** Create your own pattern with tangrams and make a drawing of it.

Parallelograms, Rectangles, Squares, and Rhombuses **59**

Parallelograms, Rectangles, Squares, and Rhombuses

Name _____   **Date** _____

▶ **Explore Parallelograms**

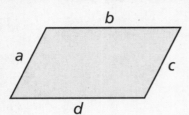

1. Write what you know about the **opposite** sides of a **parallelogram**.

_____

_____

2. Draw three different parallelograms.

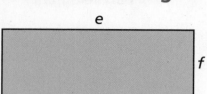

Vocabulary
rectangle
adjacent

▶ Review Rectangles

e

h   *f*

g

3. Write everything you know about the opposite sides of a **rectangle**.

_____

4. What do you know about the **adjacent** sides of a rectangle?

_____

5. Draw three different rectangles on the grid.

▶Describe Quadrilaterals

Place a check mark beside every name that describes the figure.

1.

☐ quadrilateral
☐ parallelogram
☐ rhombus
☐ rectangle
☐ square

2.

☐ quadrilateral
☐ parallelogram
☐ rhombus
☐ rectangle
☐ square

3.

☐ quadrilateral
☐ parallelogram
☐ rhombus
☐ rectangle
☐ square

4.

☐ quadrilateral
☐ parallelogram
☐ rhombus
☐ rectangle
☐ square

5.

☐ quadrilateral
☐ parallelogram
☐ rhombus
☐ rectangle
☐ square

6.

☐ quadrilateral
☐ parallelogram
☐ rhombus
☐ rectangle
☐ square

7. For each figure, put Xs under the descriptions that are always true.

	Four sides	Both pairs of opposite sides parallel	Both pairs of opposite sides the same length	Four square corners	All sides the same length
Quadrilateral					
Parallelogram					
Rhombus					
Rectangle					
Square					

Class Activity

Use the finished chart on page 63 to complete each statement.

8. Parallelograms have all the features of quadrilaterals *plus*

_____

_____

9. Rectangles have all the features of parallelograms *plus*

_____

10. Squares have all the features of quadrilaterals *plus*

_____

_____

11. Squares have all the features of parallelograms *plus*

_____

12. Squares have all the features of rectangles *plus*

_____

▶ Draw Quadrilaterals if Possible

Draw each figure if you can. If it is impossible, explain why.

13. Draw a quadrilateral that is *not* a parallelogram.

_____

14. Draw a square that is *not* a rectangle.

_____

15. Draw a parallelogram that is *not* a rectangle.

_____

16. Draw a rectangle that is *not* a square.

_____

17. Draw a rhombus that is *not* a parallelogram.

_____

Classify Quadrilaterals

Find the perimeter of each figure. Use a centimeter ruler.

1.

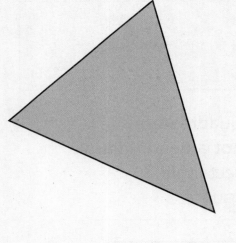

_____

2.

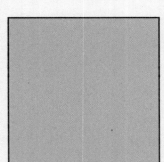

_____

Name each figure.

3.

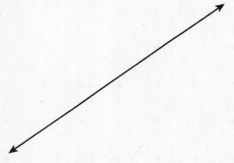

_____

4.

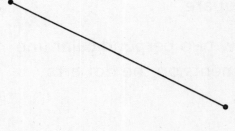

_____

Put a check mark beside every name that describes the figure.

5.

☐ quadrilateral
☐ not a quadrilateral
☐ rectangle
☐ square

6.

☐ quadrilateral
☐ not a quadrilateral
☐ rectangle
☐ square

7.

☐ quadrilateral
☐ not a quadrilateral
☐ rectangle
☐ square

8.

☐ quadrilateral
☐ not a quadrilateral
☐ rectangle
☐ square

9. Draw two perpendicular line segments on the dot array.

```
•  •  •  •  •  •  •  •  •
•  •  •  •  •  •  •  •  •
•  •  •  •  •  •  •  •  •
•  •  •  •  •  •  •  •  •
•  •  •  •  •  •  •  •  •
```

10. Extended Response Explain what it means for two line segments to be parallel. Draw an example.

_____

_____

_____

Name _____ **Date** _____

Going Further

▶ Find the Missing Digits

In each box, write the digit that makes a correct addition or subtraction.

1.
```
    ☐ 9
+   8 ☐
-------
  1 2 6
```

2.
```
  8 ☐
- ☐ 4
-------
  5 7
```

3.
```
    7 ☐
+   ☐ 8
-------
  1 3 0
```

4.
```
  1 ☐ 5
-   4 ☐
-------
    8 6
```

5.
```
    3 ☐ 9
+   ☐ 7 ☐
---------
  1 1 8 5
```

6.
```
    ☐ ☐ 5
+   3 9 ☐
---------
  ☐ 0 2 3
```

7.
```
  5 8 ☐
- ☐ ☐ 6
-------
  4 3 6
```

8.
```
  5 ☐ 7
- 2 6 ☐
-------
  ☐ 4 9
```

9.
```
  ☐ 6 4
+ 3 ☐ 8
-------
  9 5 ☐
```

10.
```
  9 ☐ 2 8
- ☐ 1 ☐ 3
---------
  4 8 5 ☐
```

11.
```
  ☐ 7 ☐ 6
+ 2 3 8 ☐
---------
  4 ☐ 4 0
```

12.
```
  6 ☐ 2 ☐
- ☐ 1 ☐ 8
---------
  3 8 2 2
```

 13. On the Back Write your own missing digit addition and missing digit subtraction.

Mixed Multi-Digit Word Problems

▶ Math and Social Studies

1. Find the difference between the height of the Statue of Liberty and the height of your teacher.

_____

2. The table shows the length of different parts of the Statue of Liberty. Fill in the table. Then find each difference.

111 ft

Length	Statue of Liberty	You	Difference
Pointing Finger	about 96 inches		
Left Hand	about 128 inches		
Right Arm	about 504 inches		

3. **Use a Calculator** There are 168 steps to climb in the Statue of Liberty. Measure how long it takes you to climb a stairway. Use that information to find out how about how long it would take you to climb to the top of the Statue of Liberty. Explain what you did.

_____

_____

_____

_____

_____

Class Activity

► **A Day at the Amusement Park**

Pedro's class is going to the amusement park.

The timeline shows how the students will spend their day.

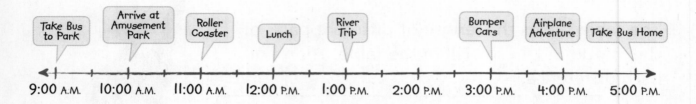

1. What time will Pedro's class go on the Airplane Adventure?

   _____

2. How long is the trip on the bus to the amusement park?

   _____

3. The students went on the Ferris wheel at 3:30 P.M. Mark that on the timeline.

4. Put these events in order starting with the earliest: Airplane Adventure, Roller Coaster, River Trip.

   _____

   _____

5. **Math Journal** Make a timeline that shows how you would like to spend the day at an amusement park. Then write two sentences about your timeline.

Use Mathematical Processes

Name _____ **Date** _____

► Review Quadrilaterals and Types of Lines

Place the letter Q on each quadrilateral. Then label each quadrilateral with the names that describe it using the letters from the Key.

Key
Parallelogram **(P)**
Rectangle **(R)**
Square **(S)**
Rhombus **(Rh)**

1.
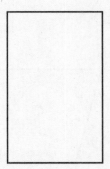

2.
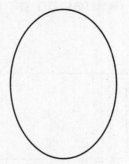

3.
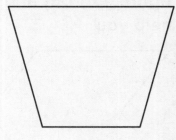

4.
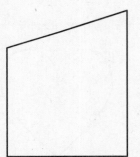

5.
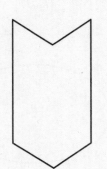

6.
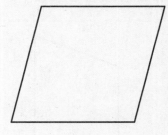

7.
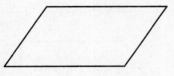

8.
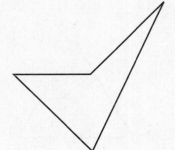

9.
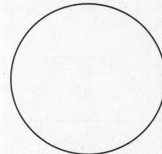

10.
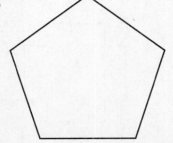

11.

12.
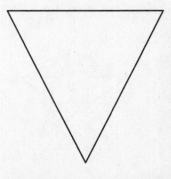

Class Activity

Vocabulary

line of symmetry

▶ Draw Lines of Symmetry

A **line of symmetry** divides a figure in half so that if you fold along the line, the two halves match each other exactly.

Draw all of the possible lines of symmetry on each figure. Cut out and fold the figures on page 101 to help you.

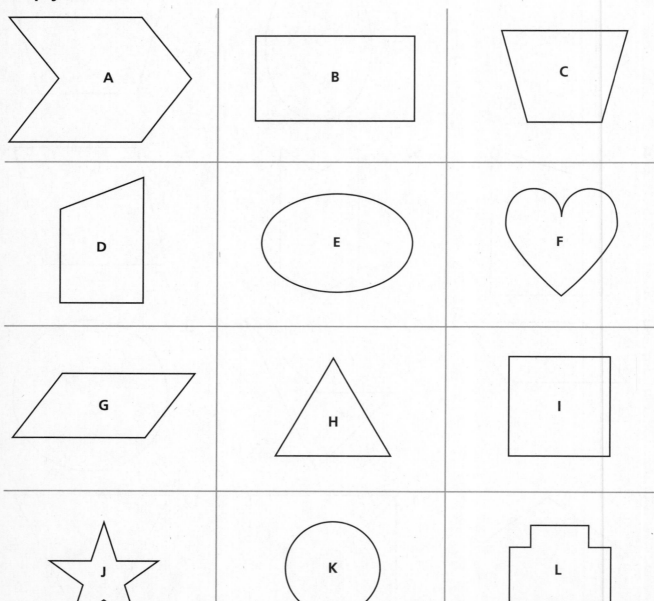

Symmetry and Congruence

Class Activity

▶ Draw Lines of Symmetry

Cut out these figures to help you with Student
Activity Book page 98.

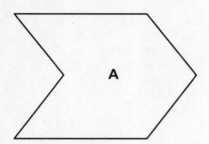

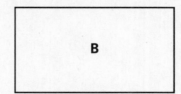

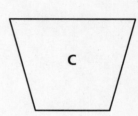

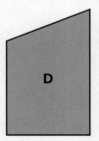

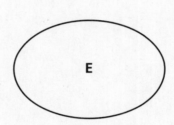

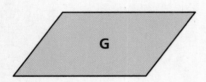

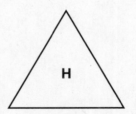

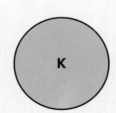

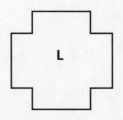

Symmetry and Congruence

Class Activity

Name _____

Date _____

Vocabulary

congruent

► Identify Congruent Halves of Figures

Two halves of a figure are **congruent** if they are the same size and shape.

Does the dashed line divide the figure into congruent halves? Write *yes* or *no*.

1.

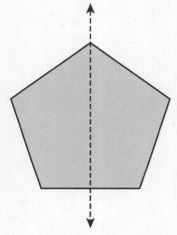

_____

2.

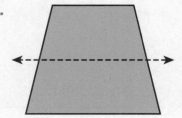

_____

3.

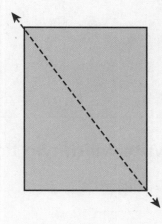

_____

4.

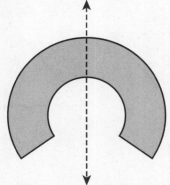

_____

5.

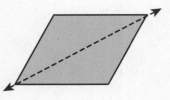

_____

6.

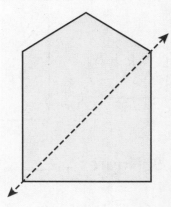

_____

Class Activity

Name _____

Date _____

Vocabulary
congruent

▶ Identify Congruent Figures

Two figures are **congruent** if they are the same size and shape. If you can slide, flip, or turn one figure so that it fits exactly on top of the other, the figures are congruent.

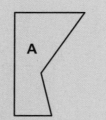 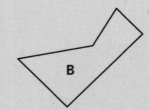

Figures A and B are congruent.

Write which two figures in each row are congruent.

7. Figures _____ and _____ are congruent.

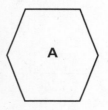 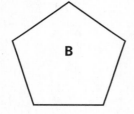 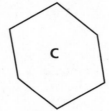

8. Figures _____ and _____ are congruent.

 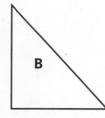  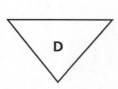 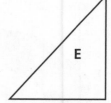

9. Figures _____ and _____ are congruent.

  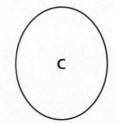 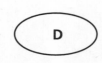

Symmetry and Congruence

4-1

Going Further

► Use Congruence and Symmetry

Solve.

1. The triangles at the right are congruent.
   Find the missing measure.

   _____

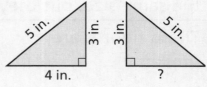

2. Complete the figure so it has the line of
   symmetry shown.

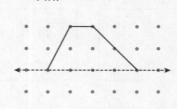

3. All parts of the two dog houses are congruent.
   How tall is Fido's dog house?

   _____

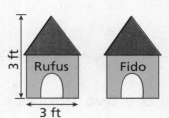

4. The lines of symmetry shown in the figure at the
   right divide the figure into congruent triangles. The
   base (short side) of one triangle measures 10 inches.
   What is the perimeter of the figure?

   _____

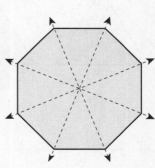

5. The rectangular field at the right has the lines
   of symmetry shown. How many feet of fencing
   are needed?

   _____

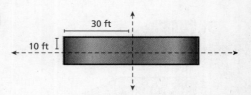

6. **Math Journal** Draw a design that has at least
   one line of symmetry and that uses at least two
   congruent figures.

Going Further

Vocabulary

similar

► Identify Similar Figures

Similar figures are the same shape. They may also be the same size, but they don't have to be.

These figures are similar.	These figures are similar.	These figures are not similar.

Are the two figures similar? Write similar or not similar.

1.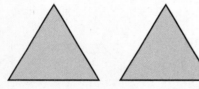

_____

2.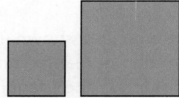

_____

3.

_____

4.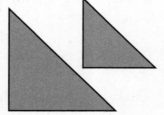

_____

Symmetry and Congruence

Dear Family,

Your child is currently participating in math activities that help him or her understand basic geometry in two dimensions.

Your child will be looking for **lines of symmetry**. If you fold a figure along a line of symmetry, the two halves will match each other exactly.

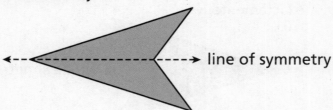

line of symmetry

Your child will also be identifying **congruent** figures. Congruent figures are the same size and shape.

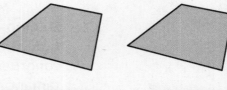

Encourage your child to look for congruent figures in your home or neighborhood and to identify lines of symmetry in various two-dimensional figures.

Your child will be learning how to label, name, and describe geometric figures. For example, the line segment *AC* is a **diagonal** of the square *ABCD*.

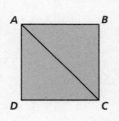

Your child will learn that angles are measured in **degrees** and discover that the sum of the measures of the angles in a triangle is always 180 degrees (180°).

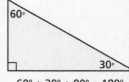

60° + 30° + 90° = 180°

If you have any questions or comments, please call or write to me.

Thank you.

Sincerely,
Your child's teacher

Estimada familia:

En estos momentos su niño o niña está participando en actividades matemáticas que le ayudan a entender la geometria básica en dos dimensiones.

Su niño o niña buscará **ejes de simetría**. Si se pliega una figura a lo largo de su eje de simetría, las dos mitades coincidirán exactamente.

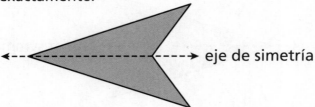

eje de simetría

Su niño o niña también identificará figuras **congruentes**. Las figuras congruentes tienen el mismo tamaño y forma.

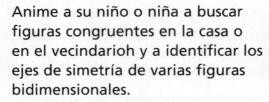

Anime a su niño o niña a buscar figuras congruentes en la casa o en el vecindarioh y a identificar los ejes de simetría de varias figuras bidimensionales.

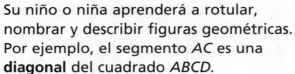

Su niño o niña aprenderá a rotular, nombrar y describir figuras geométricas. Por ejemplo, el segmento *AC* es una **diagonal** del cuadrado *ABCD*.

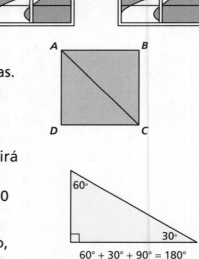

Su niño o niña aprenderá que los ángulos se miden en **grados** y descubrirá que la suma de las medidas de los ángulos de un triángulo es siempre 180 grados (180°).

Si tiene alguna pregunta o comentario, por favor comuníquese conmigo.

Gracias.

Atentamente,
El maestro de su niño

Symmetry and Congruence

Class Activity

► Label Corners with Letters

You can name figures by labeling their corners with letters.

Give two possible names for each figure.

1.

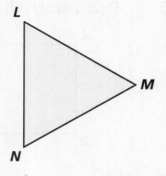

_____

_____

2.

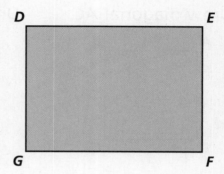

_____

3. Draw a triangle. Name it *ABC*.

4. Draw a rectangle. Name it *MNOP*.

Vocabulary
diagonal

▶ Diagonals

A line segment that connects two corners of a figure and is not a side is called a **diagonal**.

5. Draw the diagonals in the square.

Draw diagonal *AC*.	Draw diagonal *BD*.	Draw both diagonals.
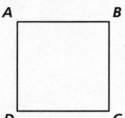	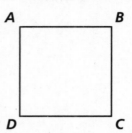	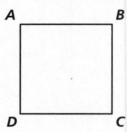

6. What do you notice about the diagonals you drew?

_____

7. What do you notice about the triangles that were formed by the diagonals you drew?

_____

8. Draw the diagonals in the rectangle.

Draw diagonal *FH*.	Draw diagonal *GI*.	Draw both diagonals.
	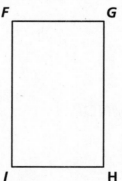	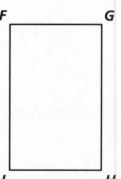

9. What do you notice about the diagonals and the triangles they formed?

_____

_____

10. Draw the diagonals in the quadrilateral.

Draw diagonal *WY*.	Draw diagonal *ZX*.	Draw both diagonals.
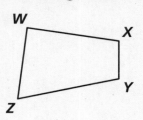	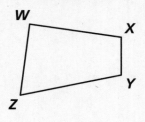	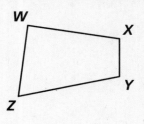

11. What do you notice about the diagonals you drew and the triangles they formed?

_____

_____

12. Draw the diagonals in the parallelogram.

Draw diagonal *KM*.	Draw diagonal *LN*.	Draw both diagonals.
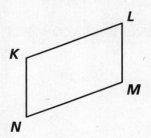	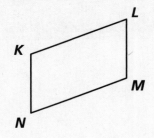	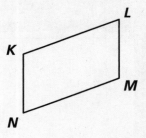

13. What do you notice about the diagonals you drew and the triangles they formed?

_____

_____

14. On the Back Draw a quadrilateral, label it, and draw all the diagonals. Name all of the sides and diagonals of your quadrilateral.

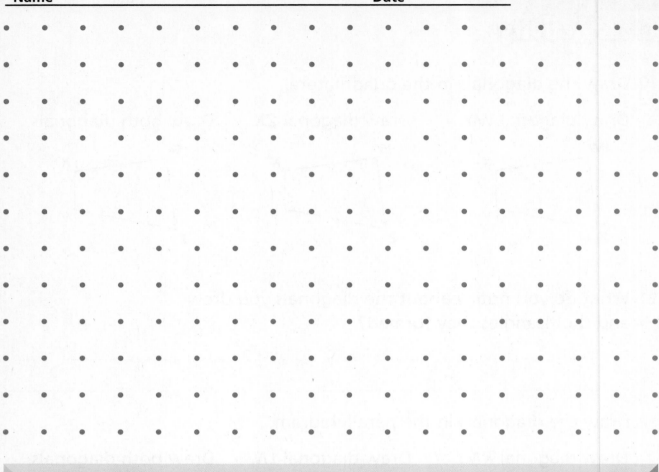

Label Figures and Draw Diagonals

▶ Types of Angles

A **ray** is part of a line that has one endpoint and continues forever in one direction. To draw a ray, make an arrow to show that it goes on forever.

Two line segments or two rays that meet at an endpoint form an **angle**.

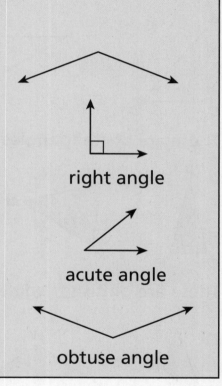

An angle that forms a square corner is called a **right angle**.

An angle that is smaller than a right angle is called an **acute angle**.

An angle that is larger than a right angle is called an **obtuse angle**.

These angles are named with a letter in the corner.

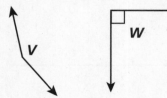
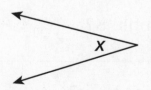

1. Which of the angles are right angles? _____

2. Which of the angles are acute angles? _____

3. Which of the angles are obtuse angles? _____

Class Activity

► ## Name Triangles by Sizes of Angles

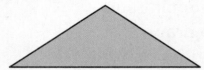 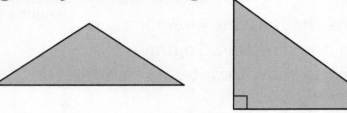

You can name triangles according to the sizes of their angles.

These are **right triangles**.

 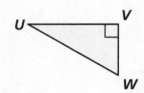 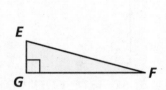 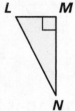

These are **acute triangles**.

 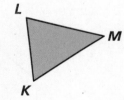 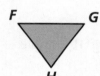 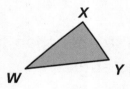

These are **obtuse triangles**.

 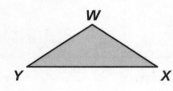  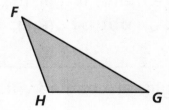

4. What do you think a right triangle is?

_____

5. What do you think an acute triangle is?

_____

6. What do you think an obtuse triangle is?

_____

Name _____ **Date** _____

Vocabulary
equilateral triangle
isosceles triangle
scalene triangle

► **Name Triangles by Lengths of Sides**

You can also name triangles according to the lengths of their sides.

These are **equilateral triangles**.

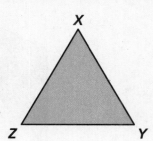

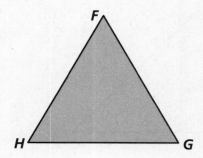

These are **isosceles triangles**.

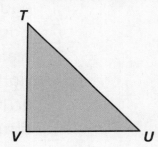
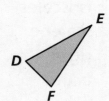
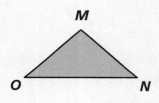

These are **scalene triangles**

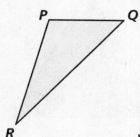
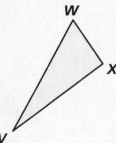
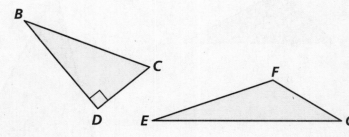

7. What do you think an equilateral triangle is?

_____

8. What do you think an isosceles triangle is?

_____

9. What do you think a scalene triangle is?

_____

Class Activity

► Name Triangles by Sizes of Angles and Lengths of Sides

Mark all the words that describe each triangle.

10.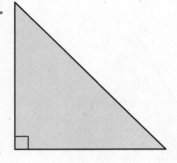

- [ ] equilateral
- [ ] isosceles
- [ ] scalene
- [ ] right
- [ ] acute
- [ ] obtuse

11.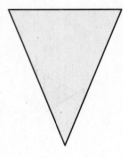

- [ ] equilateral
- [ ] isosceles
- [ ] scalene
- [ ] right
- [ ] acute
- [ ] obtuse

12.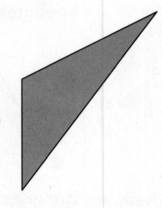

- [ ] equilateral
- [ ] isosceles
- [ ] scalene
- [ ] right
- [ ] acute
- [ ] obtuse

13.

- [ ] equilateral
- [ ] isosceles
- [ ] scalene
- [ ] right
- [ ] acute
- [ ] obtuse

14.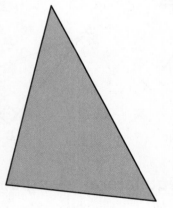

- [ ] equilateral
- [ ] isosceles
- [ ] scalene
- [ ] right
- [ ] acute
- [ ] obtuse

15.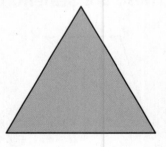

- [ ] equilateral
- [ ] isosceles
- [ ] scalene
- [ ] right
- [ ] acute
- [ ] obtuse

Name _____   **Date** _____

► Build Quadrilaterals from Triangles

Cut out each pair of triangles. Use each pair to make as many different quadrilaterals as you can. (You may flip a triangle and use the back.) On a separate piece of paper, trace each quadrilateral that you make.

Obtuse Triangles

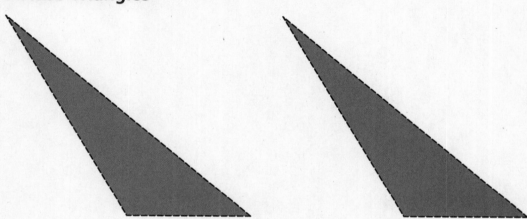

Acute Triangles

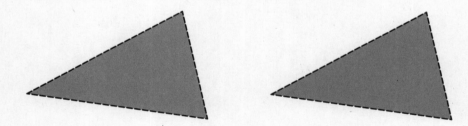

Right Triangles

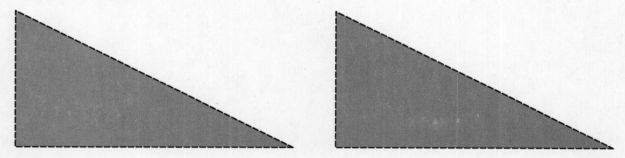

Angles and Triangles

Class Activity

Vocabulary

polygon
concave
convex

► Polygons

A **polygon** is a flat, closed figure made up of line segments that do not cross each other.

Circle the figures that are polygons.

1.

2.

3.
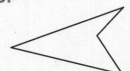

4.
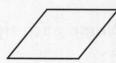

5.
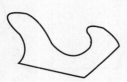

6.
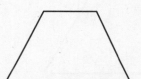

7.
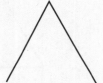

8.

A figure can be **concave** or **convex**. In concave polygons, there exists a line segment with endpoints inside the polygon and a point on the line segment that is outside the polygon. A convex figure has no such line segment.

concave   convex

Which figures are convex and which are concave?

9.

_____

10.

_____

11.
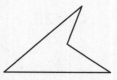

_____

12.

_____

Class Activity

Vocabulary

pentagon   hexagon
octagon   decagon

▶ Name Polygons

Polygons are named according to how many sides they have.

3 sides – **tri**angle   4 sides – **quad**rilateral   5 sides – **penta**gon

6 sides – **hexa**gon   8 sides – **octa**gon   10 sides – **deca**gon

Name each figure.

13.

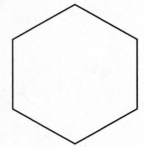

_____

14.

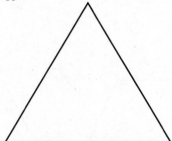

_____

15.

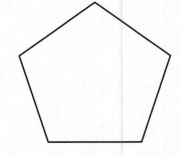

_____

16.

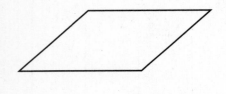

_____

17.

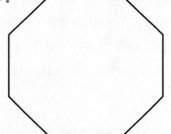

_____

18.

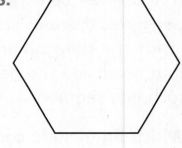

_____

19.

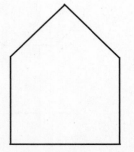

_____

20.

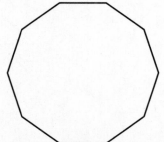

_____

21.

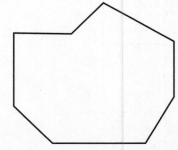

_____

▶ Build Polygons from Triangles

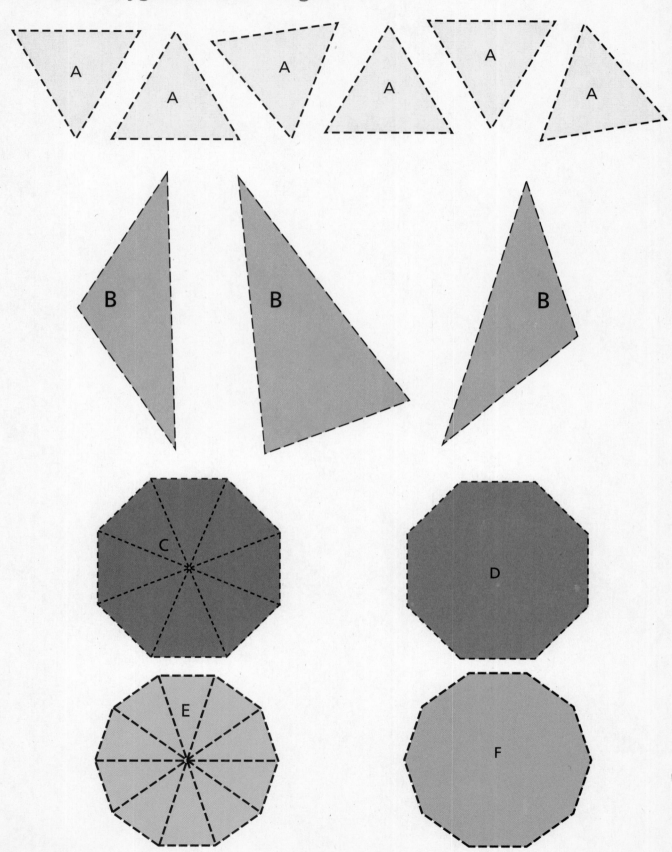

Angles and Triangles

Class Activity

Name _____ **Date** _____

Vocabulary

degree
straight angle
right angle

► Introduce Degrees

Angles are measured in units called **degrees**.
One degree is the measure of one very small rotation.

This angle has a measure of 1 degree.

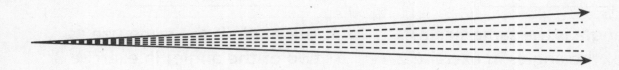

The measure of an angle is the total number of
1-degree angles that fit inside it.

This angle measures 5 degrees.

The symbol for degrees is a small raised circle (°). You
can write the measure of the angle above as 5°.

A **right angle** has a measure of 90°.
A 90°-rotation traces one quarter
of a circle.

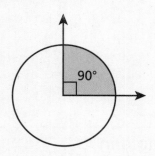

A **straight angle** measures 180°.
A 180°-rotation traces one half of
a circle.

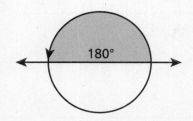

This angle measures 360°.
A 360°-rotation traces a complete
circle.

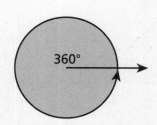

Name _____ **Date** _____

► Angle Measures

Find the size of each angle.

1. This angle is half the size of a right angle.

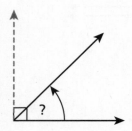

_____

2. If you put three of these angles together, you will get a right angle.

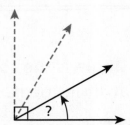

_____

3. This angle is the same size as two of the angles in exercise 2 put together.

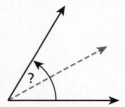

_____

4. This angle is the same size as two of the angles in exercise 3 put together.

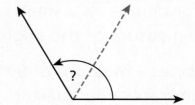

_____

5. This angle is the angle in exercise 1 added to a right angle.

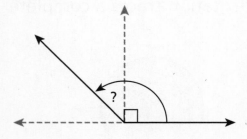

_____

6. This angle is the angle in exercise 2 added to a straight angle.

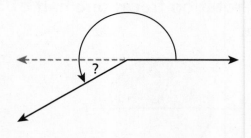

_____

Angle Measures

Class Activity

► Join Angles of a Triangle

Draw a large triangle on a sheet of unlined paper. You can draw any type of triangle. Mark each corner with a dot and then cut out the triangle.

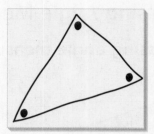

Tear each angle off the triangle, and place the three angles together so that the dotted corners are touching.

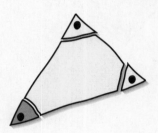

7. Sketch your three angles joined at the dotted corners.

8. What kind of angle is formed when you put together the three angles of your triangle?

   _____

Compare your sketch with those of your classmates.

9. Is the sum of the measures of the three angles the same for every triangle?

   _____

Complete this statement.

10. The sum of the measures of the three angles in a triangle is _____.

Name _____ **Date** _____

Class Activity

▶ Find Missing Angle Measures

Find the missing angle measure in each triangle.

11.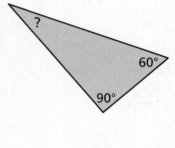

_____

12.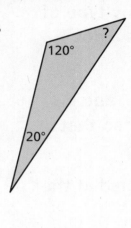

_____

13.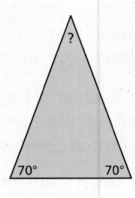

_____

14.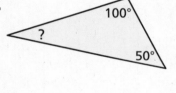

_____

15.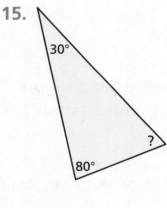

_____

16.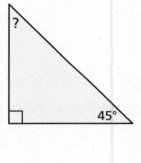

_____

17. In an equilateral triangle, each angle has the same measure. What is the measure of each angle in this equilateral triangle? _____

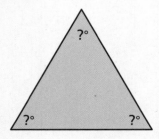

Angle Measures

1. Which two figures below are congruent?

   Figures _____ and _____ are congruent.

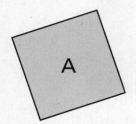

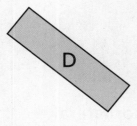

2. Draw all the lines of symmetry on the figure.

3. Draw diagonal *AC* in the rectangle.

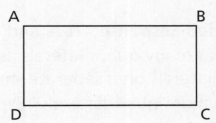

Place a check mark next to all of the words that describe the triangle.

4.

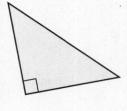

☐ equilateral
☐ isosceles
☐ scalene
☐ right
☐ acute
☐ obtuse

5.

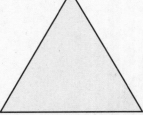

☐ equilateral
☐ isosceles
☐ scalene
☐ right
☐ acute
☐ obtuse

6.

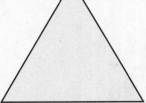

☐ equilateral
☐ isosceles
☐ scalene
☐ right
☐ acute
☐ obtuse

Place a check mark beside the words that describe the figure.

7.

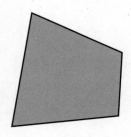

- [ ] quadrilateral
- [ ] parallelogram
- [ ] concave
- [ ] polygon

8.

- [ ] hexagon
- [ ] pentagon
- [ ] concave
- [ ] convex

9.

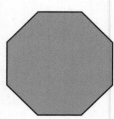

- [ ] hexagon
- [ ] convex
- [ ] polygon
- [ ] octagon

10. **Extended Response** Trace and cut out each pair of congruent triangles. Make as many quadrilaterals as you can from each pair. Trace the quadrilaterals on a separate sheet of paper. Which pair of triangles makes more quadrilaterals? Explain why.

Isosceles triangles

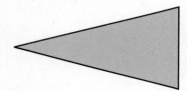

Equilateral triangles

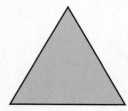 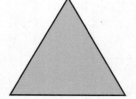

_____

_____

_____

Dear Family,

Your child has started a new unit on using addition and subtraction. These are important math operations that we use almost every day.

At the beginning of the unit, students learn to estimate sums and differences by rounding numbers. They also use estimates to check that actual answers are reasonable, and compare numbers using the symbols for greater than ($>$), less than ($<$), or equal to ($=$).

$$78 > 35 \qquad 114 < 25 + 175 \qquad 14 + 16 = 15 + 15$$

Students also identify and compare the values of a collection of U.S. coins and bills, act out making purchases by counting out the exact amounts, and find out how much change they should receive when giving more than the exact amount for a purchase.

$$66¢ \quad > \quad 41¢$$

Later in the unit, students learn to recognize word problems that contain hidden, extra, and not enough information. They solve problems with two or more steps and learn to analyze information when it is presented in tables and graphs.

Your child is learning how math is used in the world around us. You can help your child learn by sharing shopping situations with them and pointing out graphs and tables in the newspaper or magazines. Encourage your child to spend time acting out shopping situations with coins and bills at home.

Thank you for helping your child learn important math skills.

Sincerely,
Your child's teacher

Estimada familia:

Su niño ha comenzado una nueva unidad sobre suma y resta. Éstas son operaciones matemáticas importantes que usamos casi todos los días.

Al principio de esta unidad los estudiantes aprenden a estimar sumas y diferencias redondeando números. También usan la estimación para comprobar que las respuestas que dieron son razonables y comparan números usando los símbolos *mayor que* (>), *menor que* (<) o *igual* (=).

$$78 > 35 \qquad 114 < 25 + 175 \qquad 14 + 16 = 15 + 15$$

Los estudiantes también identifican y comparan los valores de una colección de monedas y billetes de los EE.UU., representan compras contando las cantidades exactas y aprenden cuánto cambio deben recibir cuando dan más de la cantidad exacta durante una compra.

$$66¢ \quad > \quad 41¢$$

Más adelante en esta unidad, los estudiantes aprenden a reconocer problemas verbales que contienen información implícita, exceso o falta de información. Resuelven problemas de dos o más pasos y aprenden a analizar la información presentada en tablas y gráficas.

Su niño está aprendiendo cómo se usan las matemáticas en la vida diaria. Usted puede ayudar a su niño compartiendo situaciones de compra y señalando gráficas y tablas en periódicos o revistas. Anime a su niño a representar en casa situaciones de compra con monedas y billetes.

Gracias por ayudar a su niño a aprender destrezas matemáticas importantes.

Atentamente,
El maestro de su niño

Round to the Nearest Hundred

Class Activity

► Coin Equivalents

What relationships do you see in this coin chart?

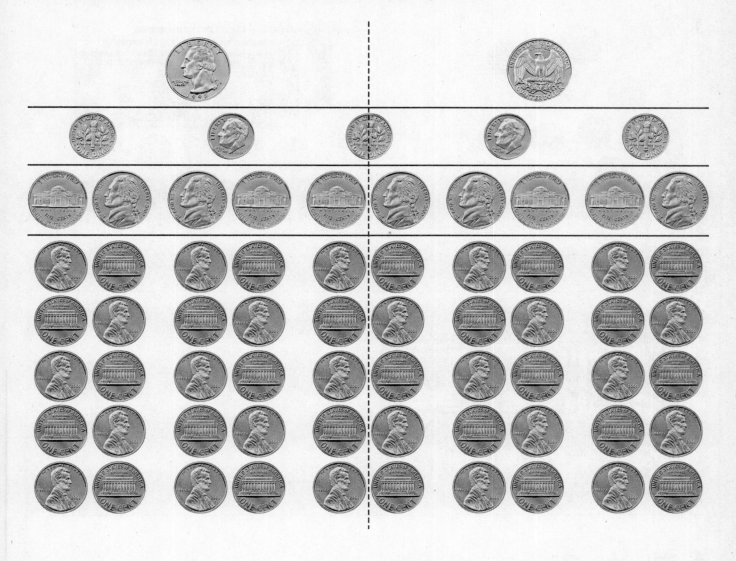

_____

_____

_____

_____

_____

►Count Coins and Bills

Find the value of each collection of coins and bills.

1.

_____

2.

_____

3.

_____

4.

_____

Money Values

Class Activity

Name _____ **Date** _____

▶ Compare Amounts of Money

Compare the two collections of coins and bills.
Write >, <, or = in the answer box.

5.

6.

7.

▶ Solve Problems Involving Money

Solve each problem.

8. Kevin wants to buy a book that costs $1.50. He has 3 quarters, 6 nickels, and 4 pennies. Does he have enough money to buy the book?

_____

9. Jade has 7 nickels, 2 dimes, and 5 quarters. Elias has 8 dimes, 6 pennies, 2 quarters, and 3 nickels. Who has more money?

_____

10. **On the Back** Explain how you solved problem 8.

Money Values

Class Activity

Name _____ Date _____

▶ Coins that Make a Dollar

Look at the two different combinations of coins that make a dollar. Can you think of some other coin combinations that make a dollar?

 =

▶ Coin Combinations

Draw two different coin combinations for each amount.

1. 37¢

2. $0.75

Draw each amount with the *fewest* coins. Use quarters, dimes, nickels, or pennies.

3. $0.88

4. $0.43

5. 71¢

6. $.95

These items are for sale at Snappy School Supplies:

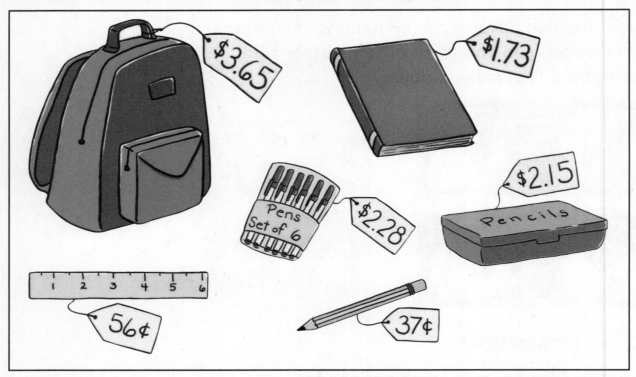

►Act It Out

You and your partner can take turns being the customer and the shopkeeper. Here's what to do:

Step 1: The customer chooses two or three items to buy.

Step 2: The shopkeeper writes down the prices and finds the total cost.

Step 3: The customer pays the exact amount of money for the items.

Step 4: The shopkeeper counts the money to make sure it is the right amount and draws the coins and bill used.

Show your work on a separate sheet of paper.

Represent Money Amounts in Different Ways

Class Activity

▶ Count On to Make Change

Imagine you are working at a sandwich shop. A customer pays for a sandwich that costs $2.78 with a $5 bill. Your cash register is broken and you don't have a pencil. How can you figure out how much change to give the customer?

Start with $2.78. Count on until you get a whole-dollar amount, and then count on by whole dollars until you get to $5.00.

$2.78 ⬤ ⬤ ⬤ ⬤   [bills]

　　　$2.79 $2.80 $2.90 $3.00 $4.00 　$5.00

Add the coins and bills to find the total amount of change, $2.22.

▶ Practice Making Change

Find the amount of change by counting on to the amount paid. Draw the coins and bills you counted.

1. Fernando paid for a $1.39 bottle of juice with two $1 bills. How much change did he get? _____

2. At a garage sale, Ana bought a $3.53 CD with a $5 bill. How much change did she get? _____

3. Valerie bought a $2.12 magazine with three $1 bills. How much change did she get? _____

Class Activity

The following items are for sale at the Beach Snack Shop:

►Act It Out

You and your partner can take turns being the customer and the shopkeeper. Here's what to do:

Step 1: The customer chooses two items to buy.

Step 2: The shopkeeper writes down the prices and finds the total cost.

Step 3: The customer pays with bills only.

Step 4: The shopkeeper counts on to find the change. Then the shopkeeper writes down the bills used to pay and the amount of change.

Show your work on a separate sheet of paper.

Make Change

▶ Round Amounts of Money

Round each amount first to the nearest dime and then to the nearest dollar.

	Rounded to the nearest dime	Rounded to the nearest dollar
1. $3.62	_____	_____
2. $5.09	_____	_____
3. $1.25	_____	_____
4. $2.99	_____	_____
5. $7.50	_____	_____

Solve each problem.

Show your work.

6. Carl spent $3.35 on a sandwich and $1.85 on a drink. Estimate the total amount he spent by rounding the prices to the nearest dollar and adding.

_____

7. Rose spent 85¢ on a pen, 32¢ on an eraser, and 78¢ on a pencil sharpener. Estimate the total amount she spent by rounding the prices to the nearest dime and adding.

_____

8. Aisha spent $4.12 on a book, $3.65 on a magazine, and $1.75 on a greeting card. Estimate the total amount she spent by rounding the prices to the nearest dollar and adding.

_____

Class Activity

► **Estimate with Money**

Jess brought $5.00 to the store. She wants to buy the items shown at the right. She needs to make an estimate to see if she has enough money.

9. Estimate the total cost of the items by rounding each price to the nearest dollar and adding. Is your estimate $5.00 or less?

_____

10. Find the actual cost of the items. Does Jess have enough money to buy the items?

_____

11. How could Jess make an estimate to be sure she has enough money?

_____

_____

Ben has $3.28. Faiz has $1.63. They want to combine their money to buy a model car that costs $5.00.

12. Estimate the total amount the boys have by rounding each amount to the nearest dollar and adding. Is your estimate $5.00 or more?

_____

13. Find the actual total amount the boys have. Do they have enough to buy the model?

_____

14. How could the boys make an estimate to be sure they have enough money?

_____

_____

Round Money Amounts

Name _____ **Date** _____

Class Activity

Solve each problem.

Tang has $1.20. He wants to buy the items shown at the right. He wants to estimate the total cost of the items to make sure he has enough money.

Tom's Toy Store

37¢ 12¢ 29¢ 18¢ 10¢

15. How do you think Tang should make his estimate? What estimate do you get if you use your method?

_____

_____

_____

16. Can Tang be sure he has enough money to buy the toys?

_____

Lidia is selling the items shown at the right at a garage sale. She wants to estimate how much money she will make to be sure she will have enough to buy a video game that costs $10.

Lidia's Garage Sale

Sweet treats Game $2.35
Sweet treats
$2.80
$4.75

17. How do you think Lidia should make her estimate? What estimate do you get if you use your method?

_____

_____

_____

18. Can Lidia be sure she will have enough money?

_____

Name _____ **Date** _____

Going Further

▶ Different Ways to Estimate with Money

Notebook $3.31

69¢

$5.89

Estimate the total cost of the notebook, marker, and baseball cap using the strategies given below.

Round to the nearest dollar	Use Mental Math
1.	2.

Complete.

3. What is the actual cost of the notebook, marker, and baseball cap? Use your estimates above to check that your answer is reasonable.

_____

4. What estimation strategy would you use to estimate the cost of several items when shopping? Explain.

_____

_____

_____

Round Money Amounts

Name _____ **Date** _____

► Read a Table

Vocabulary

table
row
cell
column

The Riverside School is taking orders for pizzas to raise money for field trips. This **table** shows the number of orders the third graders took for each type of pizza.

Third Graders' Pizza Orders

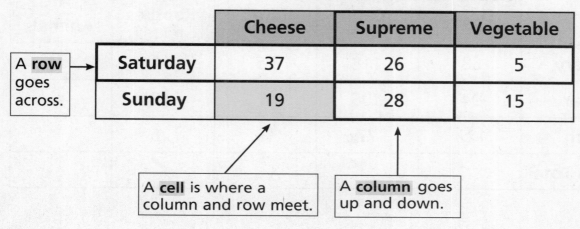

	Cheese	Supreme	Vegetable
Saturday	37	26	5
Sunday	19	28	15

A **row** goes across.

A **cell** is where a column and row meet.

A **column** goes up and down.

Use the table above to answer the questions.

Show your work.

1. How many cheese pizzas were ordered on Sunday?

   _____

2. How many vegetable pizzas were ordered on Saturday?

   _____

3. How many supreme pizzas were ordered altogether?

   _____

4. How many pizzas were ordered on Sunday?

   _____

►**Use a Table**

This table shows the number of animals a veterinarian treated over three months.

Animals Treated

	Dogs	Cats	Birds	Reptiles	All Animals
January	68	118	25	11	
February	94	106	8	19	
March	122	77	19	26	
3-Month Total					

5. Fill in the total for each column and row.

6. Write two addition questions about this table.

_____

_____

_____

_____

_____

7. Write two subtraction questions about this table.

_____

_____

_____

_____

_____

Ask Addition and Subtraction Questions from Tables

Going Further

▶Find a Pattern in a Table

Complete the tables and answer the questions.

Blocks in a Tower

Row 1	Row 2	Row 3	Row 4	Row 5	Row 6	Row 7
8 Blocks		6 Blocks	5 Blocks	4 Blocks		

1. What pattern did you use to complete the table?

_____

Money in Savings Account

Week 1	Week 2	Week 3	Week 4	Week 5	Week 6	Week 7
$300	$285		$255	$240		

2. If the pattern continues, how much money do you predict
will be in the savings account in week 8? Explain.

_____

Water Level in Tank

	Hour 1	Hour 2	Hour 3	Hour 4	Hour 5	Hour 6
Tank A	4 in.	5 in.		7 in.	8 in.	
Tank B	6 in.	8 in.	10 in.		14 in.	

3. How would you describe the pattern for each tank?

_____

_____

4. Math Journal Create your own table with a pattern.
Describe the pattern.

Going Further

Vocabulary

function table

rule

▶Function Tables

Complete each function table.

5.

Rule: Add 7	
Input	**Output**
12	19
25	
32	
54	
68	
73	

6.

Rule: Add 45	
Input	**Output**
45	90
15	
80	
100	
125	
255	

7.

Rule: Subtract 16	
Input	**Output**
36	20
48	
88	
100	
126	
159	

Write the rule for each function table.

8.

Rule: _____	
Input	**Output**
20	40
35	55
50	70
65	85
100	120
250	270

9.

Rule: _____	
Input	**Output**
15	5
20	10
38	28
57	47
110	100
212	202

10.

Rule: _____	
Input	**Output**
1	16
15	30
40	55
65	80
90	105
120	135

11.

Rule: _____						
Input	100	85	70	65	52	43
Output	95	80	65	60	47	38

Ask Addition and Subtraction Questions from Tables

Name _____ **Date** _____

►Analyze Tables

This table shows the number of people who went on different rides at an amusement park.

Number of People Who Went on Rides

	Roller Coaster	Ferris Wheel	Bumper Cars
Monday	383	237	185
Tuesday	459	84	348
Wednesday	106	671	215

Use the table above to answer the questions.

1. What do the numbers in the row for Tuesday stand for?

   _____

   _____

   _____

2. What do the numbers in the column for bumper cars stand for?

   _____

   _____

   _____

3. Find the cell with 106 in it. What does this number stand for?

   _____

   _____

   _____

▶ Fill in the Tables

4. This table shows the number of loaves of bread baked and sold last week at the Lotsa Dough Bakery. Fill in the empty cells.

Bread Sales at Lotsa Dough Bakery

	Loaves Baked	Loaves Sold	Loaves Left
Monday	122	38	
Tuesday	113	47	
Wednesday	145		89
Thursday		96	38
Friday	91		44

5. This table shows the number of CDs and videotapes sold at the Sound Out Music Store last week. Fill in the empty cells.

Sound Out Music Sales

	CDs	Videotapes	Total
Monday	62	19	81
Tuesday	73	32	
Wednesday	88		133
Thursday		26	120
Friday	155		223
Saturday		66	294

Complete Tables

►Use Deductive Reasoning

Solve each problem.

1. Jan, Bev, Luis, and Alex are wearing different color caps. The colors are red, blue, green, and yellow. Jan's cap is not red or green. Alex's cap is red. Bev's cap is not green or yellow. What color cap is each wearing?

	Red	Blue	Green	Yellow
Jan				
Bev				
Luis				
Alex				

2. Ty, Sal, Amy, and Lea were in a race. Amy did not finish either first or second. Lea finished last. Sal finished before Ty. In what order did they finish the race?

	First	Second	Third	Fourth
Ty				
Sal				
Amy				
Lea				

3. Mai, Abdul, Bill, and Rita each play different instruments. The instruments are violin, flute, harp, and guitar. Mai's instrument does not have strings. Bill plays the violin. Abdul does not play the harp. What does each person play?

	violin	flute	harp	guitar
Mai				
Abdul				
Bill				
Rita				

4. **Math Journal** Create your own problem like the ones above.

Going Further

▶ Use Inductive Reasoning

5. Look for a pattern in the lines of symmetry inside the squares below and the number of triangles formed by them. How many triangles will there be in a square with three lines of symmetry? four lines of symmetry? _____

6. Eight baseball teams will play each of the other teams once. Use a pattern to find how many games will take place? _____

| 2 teams | 3 teams | 4 teams | 5 teams |

| 1 game | 3 games | 6 games | 10 games |

7. Describe the pattern you used to find the answer to Problem 6.

_____

8. Connect the six dots using just three line segments. Do not lift your pencil from the paper or retrace any line segment. The dashed line segments show you a way to start.

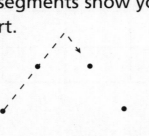

9. Connect all nine dots using just four line segments. Do not lift your pencil from the paper or retrace any line segment.

· · ·

· · ·

· · ·

10. Is there a pattern that you could use to solve Problems 8 and 9? _____

Complete Tables

►Make a Table

Use the data the class collected to fill in the table.

►Use a Table

1. Write a comparison question using data from the table above and the word *more.* Answer your question.

_____

_____

2. Write a comparison question using data from the table above and the word *fewer.* Answer your question.

_____

_____

3. Write a question using data from the table and the word *altogether.* Answer your question.

_____

_____

Class Activity

Name _____ Date _____

►Analyze Data

Fill in the missing information in the tables and answer the questions.

This table shows the number of souvenirs the Wildcats baseball team sold last weekend.

Souvenir Sales for Wildcats Baseball Team

	White	Red	Total
Caps	134		211
T-shirts	64	109	
Pennants	59		151

4. Which item above had the most total sales? _____

5. Which color T-shirt had the most sales? _____

This table shows the number of items the Green Thumb Garden Shop sold at their Spring sale.

Spring Sale at Green Thumb Garden Shop

	Number Before the Sale	Number Sold	Number Left
Spades	232	185	
Straw Hats		68	76
Small Pots	412		70
Big Pots		227	98

6. Which item had the most sales? _____

7. Which item has the least number left? _____

More Practice With Tables

Class Activity

Name _____ Date _____

▶Read a Pictograph

A **pictograph** is a graph that uses pictures or symbols to represent data. The pictograph below shows the number of votes for favorite ice cream flavors.

Favorite Ice Cream Flavors

Peanut Butter Crunch	🍦
Cherry Vanilla	🍦 🍦 🍦
Chocolate	🍦 🍦 🍦 🍦 🍦

Each 🍦 = 3 votes.

Use the pictograph above to answer the questions.

1. How many votes were there for chocolate?

   _____

2. How many votes were there for Cherry Vanilla?

   _____

3. How many people voted in all for their favorite ice cream flavor?

   _____

4. How many fewer votes were there for Peanut Butter Crunch than Chocolate?

   _____

▶Make a Pictograph

5. Use the data about Kanye's CDs to make your own pictograph.

Kanye's CDs	
Type	**Number of CDs**
Jazz	12
Rap	16
Classical	4

▶ Read a Horizontal Bar Graph

Look at this **horizontal bar graph** and answer the question.

Flowers in Mary's Garden

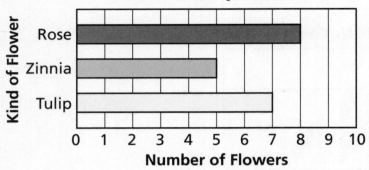

Kind of Flower: Rose, Zinnia, Tulip

Number of Flowers: 0 1 2 3 4 5 6 7 8 9 10

6. What do the bars represent?

_____

_____

_____

▶ Read a Vertical Bar Graph

Look at this **vertical bar graph** and answer the question.

Vehicles in Murray's Used Car Lot

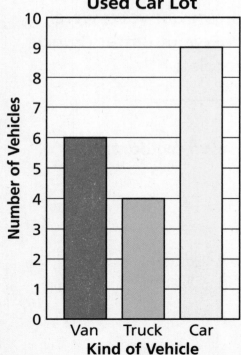

Number of Vehicles: 0 1 2 3 4 5 6 7 8 9 10

Kind of Vehicle: Van Truck Car

7. What do the bars represent?

_____

_____

_____

Read and Create Pictographs and Bar Graphs

► Create a Horizontal Bar Graph

Use the information in this table to complete the horizontal bar graph.

Balls in the Gym

Type of Ball	Number of Balls
Soccer ball	4
Basketball	6
Softball	9

8.

► Create a Vertical Bar Graph

Use the information in this table to complete the vertical bar graph.

Favorite Fruits

Type of Fruit	Number Who Chose It
Apple	5
Banana	6
Orange	4

9.

Name _____ **Date** _____

► **Take a Survey and Record Results**

| **Topics** |
| Sports |
| Animals |
| Colors |
| School Subjects |
| Snacks |

10. Choose a survey topic from the box or make up one of your own. Then take a survey to find the favorite.

Which _____ is your favorite?	
Answer Choice	**Tally**

11. Use the tally chart to complete the horizontal bar graph.

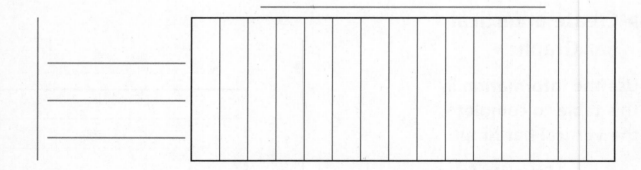

12. **Math Journal** Write two questions that can be answered using the bar graph. Then answer them.

Read and Create Pictographs and Bar Graphs

►Horizontal Bar Graphs with Multi-Digit Numbers

Use this horizontal bar graph to answer the questions below.

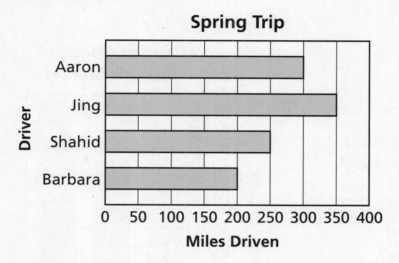

Spring Trip

1. How many miles did Shahid drive?

_____

2. Who drove the most miles?

_____

3. How many miles did Aaron and Barbara drive altogether?

_____

4. How many more miles did Jing drive than Shahid?

_____

5. How many fewer miles did Barbara drive than Jing?

_____

6. Write two more questions that can be answered by using the graph.

_____

_____

Name _____

Date _____

▶Vertical Bar Graphs with Multi-Digit Numbers

Use the vertical bar graph at the right to answer the questions below.

7. How many cans of peas are at Turner's Market?

_____

8. Which type of canned goods does Turner's Market have the least of?

_____

9. How many cans of beans and peaches are there altogether?

_____

10. How many more cans of beans are there than peas?

_____

11. How many fewer cans of peaches are there than peas?

_____

12. Write two more questions that can be answered by using the graph.

_____

_____

_____

_____

_____

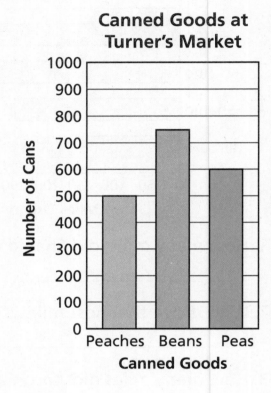

Canned Goods at Turner's Market

Read and Create Bar Graphs with Multi-Digit Numbers

► **Create a Horizontal Bar Graph with Multi-Digit Numbers**

13. Use the information in this table to make a horizontal bar graph.

Joe's Video Collection	
Type	**Videos**
Comedy	60
Action	35
Drama	20

► **Create a Vertical Bar Graph with Multi-Digit Numbers**

14. Use the information in this table to make a vertical bar graph.

Summer Bike Sales	
Type of Bike	**Number Sold**
Road Bike	200
Mountain Bike	600
Hybrid Bike	450

15. **On the Back** Write two questions that can be answered using one of the graphs.

_____

_____

_____

_____

_____

_____

_____

_____

_____

_____

_____

_____

_____

_____

Read and Create Bar Graphs with Multi-Digit Numbers

Class Activity

Name _____

Date _____

Vocabulary

tally chart
frequency table
line plot
mode
range

▶Introduce Frequency Tables and Line Plots

The ages of some players on a basketball team can be shown in different ways.

A **tally chart** can be used to record and organize data.

A **frequency table** shows how many times events occur.

A **line plot** shows the frequency of data on a number line.

Tally Chart	
Age	**Tally**
7	I
8	III
9	JHI1
10	IIII
11	II

Frequency Table	
Age	**Tally**
7	1
8	3
9	5
10	4
11	2

Line Plot

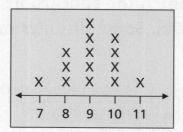

Ages of Basketball Players

▶Review Mode and Range

The **mode** is the value that appears most frequently in a set of data.

The **range** is the difference between the greatest value and the least value in a set of data.

Use the line plot above to complete exercises 1 and 2.

1. What is the mode for the set of data? _____

2. What is the range for the set of data? _____

Name _____ **Date** _____

Class Activity

▶ Match Conclusions to Data

Suppose that you work at a toy store. You show information in different displays. Below are conclusions made from displays about toy sales in three stores.

A. Store A sold more items than Store B and Store C.

B. More toys were bought in October than in January.

C. More stuffed animals were sold than any other items.

D. Most dolls purchased cost $10.

Match the conclusions above to the display that represents that data. Some displays may not match a conclusion.

3.
4–Month Toy Sales

October
November
December
January
100 200 300 400
Number of Toys

4.
2008 Toy Sales

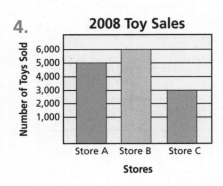

Number of Toys Sold
6,000
5,000
4,000
3,000
2,000
1,000
Store A   Store B   Store C
Stores

5.
Prices of Dolls Purchased

	X		
X	X		
X	X		
X	X		
X	X	X	
X	X	X	X
$5	$10	$15	$20

Price

6.
2008 Toy Sales

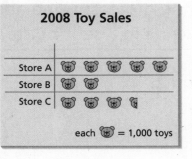

each 🐻 = 1,000 toys

7.

Weekly Doll Purchases	
Sunday	0
Monday	3
Tuesday	2
Wednesday	3
Thursday	1
Friday	4
Saturday	5

8.

2008 Toy Sales for stores A, B, and C	
Board Games	10,863
Video Games	15,829
Stuffed Animals	29,362
Books	13,256

Represent and Organize Data

Class Activity

Name _____ **Date** _____

▶ **Math and Science**

Finish

Three frogs are having a Frog Jumping Contest.
The length of the race is 1,000 cm.
The table shows how far each frog goes in 1 jump.

Name of Frog	Length of Jump
Freddie	about 200 cm
Flora	about 315 cm
Frankie	about 144 cm

Use a Calculator.

1. Bena says it will take Flora about 3 jumps to cross the finish line? Is she right?

   _____

   _____

2. What conclusions can you make about how many jumps it will take the other frogs to cross the finish line?

   _____

   _____

3. What conclusion can you make about how many of his body lengths Freddie the Frog can jump?

   _____

   _____

Freddie's Body Length

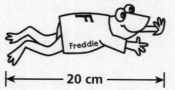

Freddie

|← 20 cm →|

Class Activity

▶ **How Far Can You Jump?**

4. Ask 10 students to jump. Measure the length of each jump. Record the names of the students and the length of the jumps in a table.

5. Make a bar graph on grid paper that shows the length of each jump. Put the data in order from shortest jump to longest jump.

6. Look at the graph you made. What is the shape of the data?

_____

7. What is the mode and range?

_____

8. What is your prediction for the jump of another student who has not jumped yet? Why do you think that is a good prediction?

_____

9. What conclusion can you make about how far the 10 students can jump?

_____

_____

Use Mathematical Processes

Compare the numbers. Write >, <, or = in each ◯.

1. 742 ◯ 724

2. 2,329 ◯ 2,319

Write the numbers in order from least to greatest.

3. 598, 678, 590

_____

4. 6,543, 7,585, 6,585

_____

Round each number to the given place.

5. 567 (nearest hundred)

_____

6. $7.89 (nearest dime)

_____

7. $6.29 (nearest dollar)

_____

Use the line plot to answer question 8.

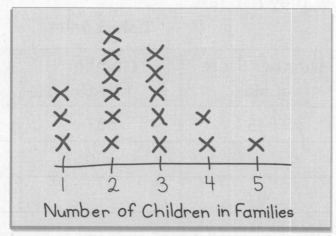

Number of Children in Families

8. What is the mode and range of the data?

mode: _____   range: _____

Use the bar graph to answer questions 9 and 10.

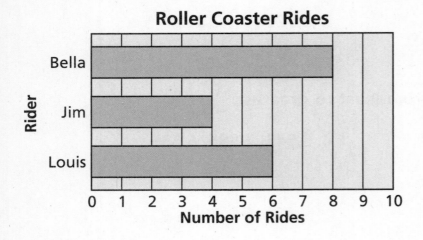

Roller Coaster Rides

9. How many more rides did Louis take than Jim? _____

10. How many rides did Bella and Louis take altogether? _____

This table shows the numbers of T-shirts of different sizes a store had before a big sale, the number they sold, and the number they had left.

T-shirt Sales

	Number Bfore Sale	Number Sold	Number Left After Sale
Small	645	587	
Medium		390	45
Large	462		29

11. Fill in the blank cells.

12. How many more small T-shirts than large T-shirts did the store have before the sale?

_____

Solve. Cross out any extra information. Circle any hidden information.

Show your work.

13. Becky has 20 fish and 2 hamsters. There are 8 angelfish and the rest of the fish are goldfish. She gets 7 more goldfish. How many goldfish does she have now?

_____

14. Raj is going on vacation for a week and 5 days. How many days will Raj be gone?

_____

Solve. Label your answer.

15. Jason has 485 toy dinosaurs in his collection. He plans to sell 243 toy dinosaurs. Round each number to the nearest ten to estimate how many he will have left.

_____

Solve the problem if possible. If more information is needed, rewrite the problem to include the necessary information and then solve it.

16. Julie and Sam grew tomato plants. Julie's plant grew 16 inches. How much taller did Sam's plant grow?

_____

_____

_____

_____

Compare the two collections of coins and bills.
Write >, <, or = in the ◯.

17.

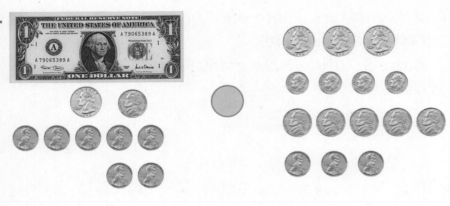

18. Draw two different coin combinations for 78¢.

Solve.

19. Uri bought a tube of toothpaste for $2.58. He
paid with a $5.00 bill. Find the amount of
change by counting on. Draw the coins and bills
you counted. How much change did he get?

Show your work.

_____

20. **Extended Response** Alexa has $5.00. She wants
to order a sandwich for $3.65 and a drink for
$1.48. How can she estimate to be sure she has
enough money? _____

_____

_____

What estimate do you get using your method?
Can Alexa be sure she has enough money to
buy the sandwich and the drink?

_____

Class Activity

Name _____

Date _____

Vocabulary
flip

▶ Draw Flips

When you **flip** a figure over a line, you get a mirror image.

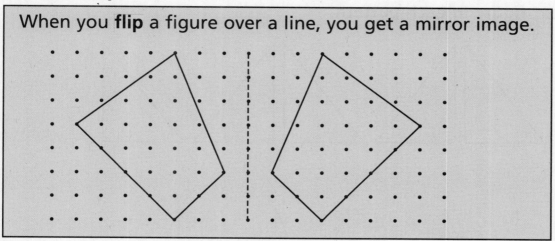

Draw the flipped image of each figure.

1.

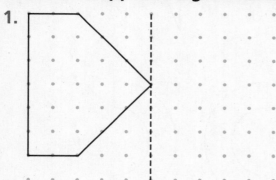

2.

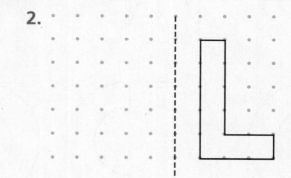

3.

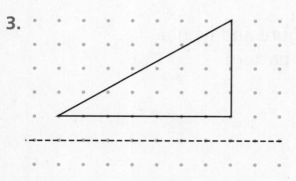

4.

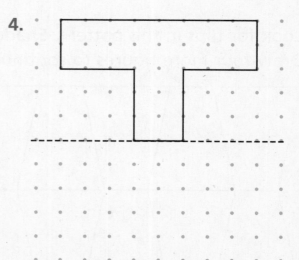

Class Activity

▶ Use Flips in Patterns

Draw the next figure in each pattern.

5.

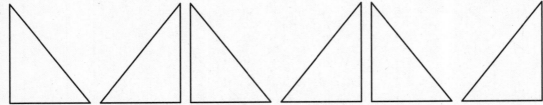

6.

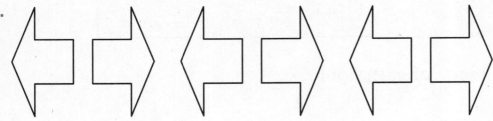

7.

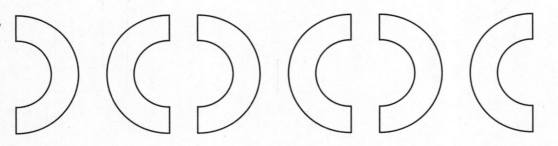

8. Look for flips in this pattern. Shade a figure and its flip.
Draw four more figures to continue the pattern.

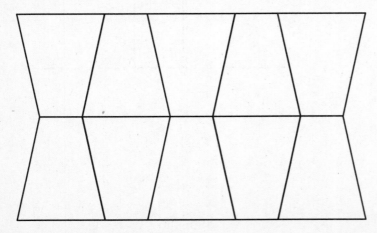

Motion Geometry Patterns

Name _____ **Date** _____

▶ Describe and Draw Slides

You can **slide** a figure along a line.

This slide moves the figure to the right and down.

This slide moves the figure up and to the right.

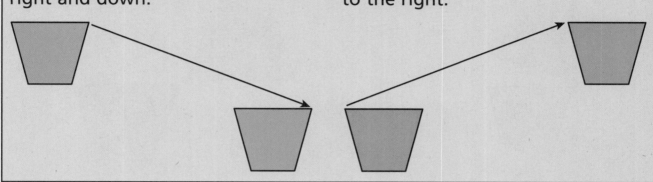

Describe each slide. Draw the new figure.

9. _____

10. _____

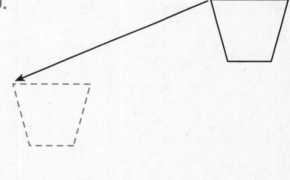

11. _____

12. _____

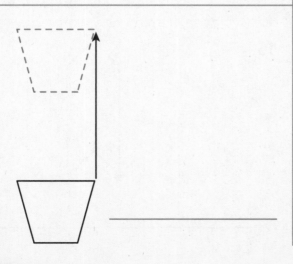

Motion Geometry Patterns **183**

Name _____ **Date** _____

Class Activity

Vocabulary

turn

▶ Describe and Draw Turns

You can **turn** a figure around a point.

This is a quarter turn.

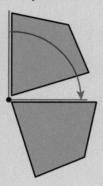

This is a half turn.

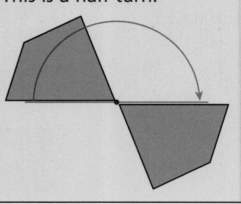

Describe each turn. Draw the new figure.

13.

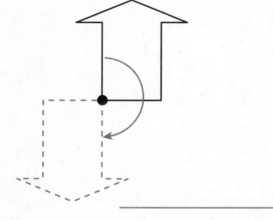

_____

14.

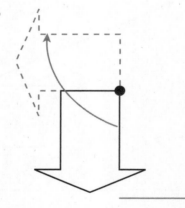

_____

15.

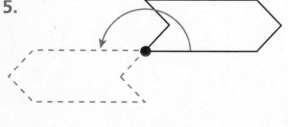

_____

16.

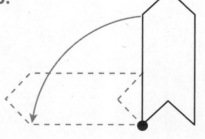

_____

Motion Geometry Patterns

Dear Family,

Your child is studying patterns that grow, patterns that shrink, and patterns that repeat. Students will find pattern rules and continue patterns for both number and geometric patterns. Students will also use patterns to solve real-world problems. Repeating patterns from geometry are used everywhere: in art, tiling designs, quilts, and clothing. Slides (translations), flips (reflections), and turns (rotations) can be used to make tiling patterns.

This diagram shows how copies of this geometric figure can fit together to make a tiling pattern.

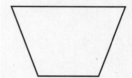

Turn the figure around a point.

Flip the figure over a line.

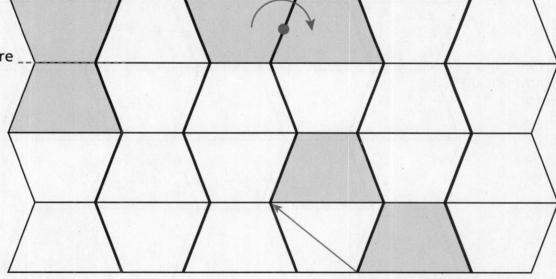

Slide the figure up and to the left.

If you have any questions or comments, please call or write to me. Thank you.

Sincerely,
Your child's teacher

Estimada familia:

La unidad que su niño está estudiando trata de patrones: patrones que aumentan, patrones que disminuyen, patrones que se repiten. Los patrones geométricos que se repiten se usan en todas partes: en arte, en diseños de azulejos, en colchas y en ropa. Los deslizamientos (traslaciones), las inversiones (reflexiones) y los giros (rotaciones), servirán para hacer patrones de azulejos.

Este diagrama muestra de qué manera pueden combinarse las copias de esta figura geométrica para formar un patrón de azulejos.

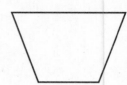

Gira la figura
sobre un punto.

Invierte la
figura por un
borde.

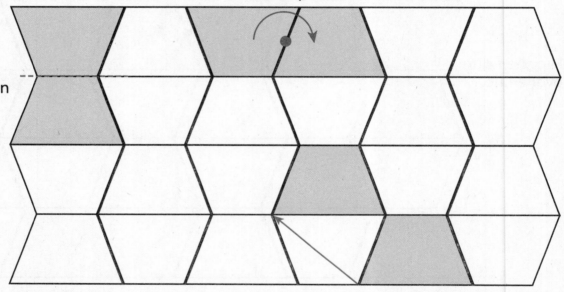

Desliza la figura hacia
arriba y la izquierda.

Si tiene alguna pregunta o comentario, por favor comuníquese conmigo. Gracias.

Atentamente,
El maestro de su niño.

Motion Geometry Patterns

Name _____

Date _____

Class Activity

▶ **Explore Repeating Number Patterns**

Sometimes a number pattern continues by repeating the same digits.

Continue each number pattern.

1. 2 7 2 7 2 7 _____

2. 1 2 2 1 2 2 1 2 2 _____

3. 1 3 2 1 3 2 1 3 2 _____

4. 1 0 0 1 1 0 0 1 1 0 0 1 _____

▶ **Explore Repeating Patterns in Skip Counting**

Complete.

5. Skip count by 2s.

2, 4, 6, 8, 10, ____ , ____ , ____ , ____ , ____ , ____ , ____ , ____

6. Show the pattern in the ones digits when you skip count by 2s, starting at 2.

____ , ____ , ____ , ____ , ____ , ____ , ____ , ____ , ____ , ____

7. Start at 1 and count by 2s.

1, 3, 5, ____ , ____ , ____ , ____ , ____ , ____ , ____

8. Show the pattern in the ones digits in exercise 7.

____ , ____ , ____ , ____ , ____ , ____ , ____ , ____ , ____ , ____

9. Skip count by 5s.

5, 10, 15, ____ , ____ , ____ , ____ , ____ , ____ , ____ , ____ , ____

10. Show the pattern in the ones digits when you skip count by 5s, starting at 5.

____ , ____ , ____ , ____ , ____ , ____ , ____ , ____

► Explore Repeating Shape Patterns

This pattern repeats the same figures over and over.
You can describe it as a triangle, flipped triangle,
square, repeat.

Draw the next figure in each pattern.

11.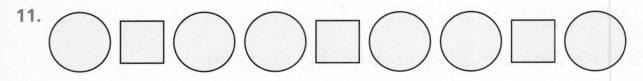

12.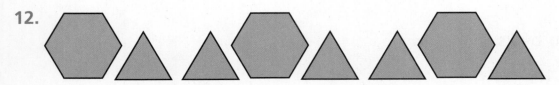

13.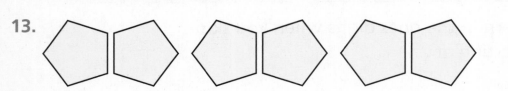

14. Show two ways to make a repeating pattern with
these starting figures.

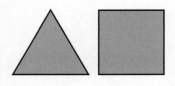

_____   _____   _____   _____

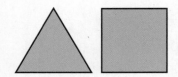

_____   _____   _____   _____

Name _____ **Date** _____

Class Activity

Vocabulary
growing pattern
shrinking pattern

▶ Continue a Growing or Shrinking Number Pattern

A number pattern can grow or shrink by the same amount.

Continue the pattern and write the rule.

1. 5, 8, 11, 14, 17, ____ , ____ , ____ , ____ , ____ , ____ , ____

_____

2. 30, 27, 24, 21, ____ , ____ , ____ , ____ , ____ , ____

_____

A number pattern can grow or shrink by a changing amount.
When this happens, look for a pattern in the changes.

Continue the pattern and write the rule.

3. 6, 7, 9, 12, 16, ____ , ____ , ____ , ____ , ____ , ____ , ____

_____

4. 2, 6, 11, 15, 20, 24, 29, ____ , ____ , ____ , ____ , ____ , ____

_____

Make two patterns with these starting numbers.
Write the rule.

5. 2, 4, ____ , ____ , ____   _____

   2, 4, ____ , ____ , ____   _____

6. 50, 45, ____ , ____ , ____   _____

   50, 45, ____ , ____ , ____   _____

▶ Number Patterns on a Calculator

7. Use a calculator to check your pattern and rule in exercises 1 and 2.

Name _____ **Date** _____

Class Activity

► Continue a Growing or Shrinking Shape Pattern

The figures in this pattern
grow larger and larger.

8. How does the pattern grow?

_____

_____

Draw the next figure in each pattern.

9.

10.

11.

12.

Growing and Shrinking Patterns

Name _____ **Date** _____

▶ Solve a Simpler Problem

How many small triangles will be in triangle number 10? One way to solve problems like this one is to solve a simpler problem and look for a pattern.

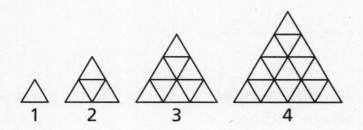

1   2   3   4

13. Complete the table to show how the number of small triangles grows.

14. Draw figure 5 in the pattern above. In the table, record the number of triangles it has.

15. Describe how the pattern grows.

_____

_____

_____

_____

Triangle Number	Number of Small Triangles
1	
2	
3	
4	
5	

16. Use this pattern to find how many small triangles are in triangle number 10. _____

Solve.

17. If 8 friends all shake hands with each other once, how many handshakes will take place?

_____

▶ Solve Real-World Problems

Use a number pattern to solve each problem.

18. One cookie costs 50¢, a bag of two cookies costs 59¢, and a bag of 3 cookies costs 68¢. If the pattern continues how much will it cost to buy a bag of 6 cookies?

_____

19. This is the window pattern on a building. How many windows will be in the pattern if there are 7 floors?

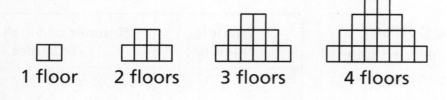

| 1 floor | 2 floors | 3 floors | 4 floors |

_____

20. A floor has this tile pattern. If there are 4 rings around the center, how many tiles will there be in all?

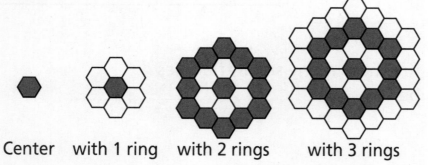

Center   with 1 ring   with 2 rings   with 3 rings

_____

Growing and Shrinking Patterns

1. Is the second figure the result of a slide, flip, or turn?

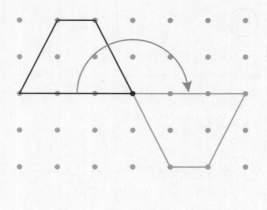

_____

2. Draw the next figure in the pattern.

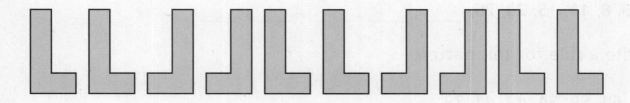

3. Continue the number pattern.

329329329329329 _____

4. Draw the next figure in the pattern.

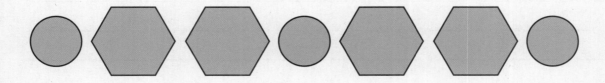

5. Write a rule for this pattern.

_____

6. Continue this pattern.

65, 62, 59, 56, 53, 50, 47, _____ , _____ , _____ , _____ , _____

7. Continue this pattern.

12, 16, 20, 24, 28, 32, 36, _____ , _____ , _____ , _____ , _____

8. Continue this pattern.

5, 6, 8, 11, 15, 20, 26, _____ , _____ , _____ , _____ , _____

9. Write a rule for this pattern.

69, 64, 59, 54, 49, 44, 39

_____

10. **Extended Response** In September, Elisa walks dogs for $1.25 per walk. In October, she charges $1.50 per walk. In November, she charges $1.75 per walk. If the pattern continues, how much will she charge per walk in December and January? Describe the pattern rule you used to solve the problem.

_____

_____

_____

_____

Class Activity

▶ Explore Patterns with 5s

What patterns do you see below?

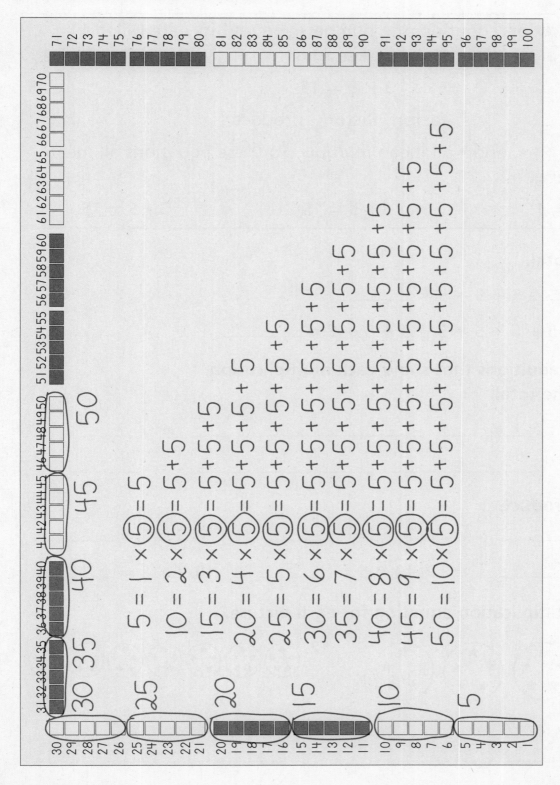

$$5 = 1 \times 5 = 5$$
$$10 = 2 \times 5 = 5 + 5$$
$$15 = 3 \times 5 = 5 + 5 + 5$$
$$20 = 4 \times 5 = 5 + 5 + 5 + 5$$
$$25 = 5 \times 5 = 5 + 5 + 5 + 5 + 5$$
$$30 = 6 \times 5 = 5 + 5 + 5 + 5 + 5 + 5$$
$$35 = 7 \times 5 = 5 + 5 + 5 + 5 + 5 + 5 + 5$$
$$40 = 8 \times 5 = 5 + 5 + 5 + 5 + 5 + 5 + 5 + 5$$
$$45 = 9 \times 5 = 5 + 5 + 5 + 5 + 5 + 5 + 5 + 5 + 5$$
$$50 = 10 \times 5 = 5 + 5 + 5 + 5 + 5 + 5 + 5 + 5 + 5 + 5$$

Multiply with 5 **195**

Class Activity

▶ Practice Multiplications with 5

Vocabulary

multiplication
factor
product

In a **multiplication** equation, the numbers you multiply are called **factors**. The answer, or total, is the **product**.

$$3 \times 5 = 15$$

factor   factor   product

The symbols ×, *, and • all mean *multiply*. So these equations all mean the same thing.

$3 \times 5 = 15$ $3 * 5 = 15$ $3 • 5 = 15$

Write each total.

1. $4 \times \boxed{5} = 5 + 5 + 5 + 5 = $ _____

2. $7 • \boxed{5} = 5 + 5 + 5 + 5 + 5 + 5 + 5 = $ _____

Write the 5s additions that show each multiplication. Then write the total.

3. $6 \times \boxed{5} = $ _____ $= $ _____

4. $9 * \boxed{5} = $ _____ $= $ _____

Write each product.

5. $8 \times 5 = $ _____   6. $2 \times 5 = $ _____   7. $5 \times 5 = $ _____

8. $4 \times 5 = $ _____   9. $10 \times 5 = $ _____   10. $7 \times 5 = $ _____

Write a 5s multiplication equation for each picture.

11.

12.

_____   _____

Multiply with 5

Dear Family,

In this unit and the next, your child will be practicing basic multiplications and divisions. *Math Expressions* incorporates studying, practicing, and testing of the basic multiplications and divisions in class. Your child is also expected to practice at home.

Study Plans Each day your child will fill out a study plan, indicating which basic multiplications and divisions he or she will study that evening. When your child has finished studying (practicing), his or her Homework Helper should sign the study plan.

4–1	Name	Date
Homework		

Study Plan

5s count bys
5s multiplications

_____

Homework Helper

Practice Charts Each time a new number is introduced, students' homework will include a practice chart. To practice, students can cover the products with a pencil or a strip of heavy paper. They will say the multiplications, sliding the pencil or paper down the column to see each product after saying it. Students can also start with the last problem in a column and slide up. It is important that your child studies count-bys and multiplications at least 5 minutes every night. Your child can also use these charts to practice division on the mixed up column by covering the first factor.

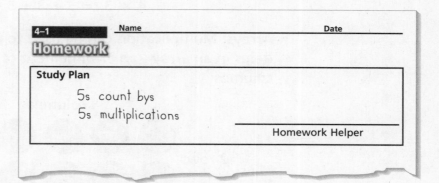

	In Order	Mixed Up
	1 × 5 = 5	9 × 5 = 45
	2 × 5 = 10	5 × 5 = 25
	3 × 5 = 15	2 × 5 = 10
	4 × 5 = 20	7 × 5 = 35
5s	5 × 5 = 25	4 × 5 = 20
	6 × 5 = 30	6 × 5 = 30
	7 × 5 = 35	10 × 5 = 50
	8 × 5 = 40	8 × 5 = 40
	9 × 5 = 45	1 × 5 = 5
	10 × 5 = 50	3 × 5 = 15

To help students understand the concept of multiplication, the *Math Expressions* program presents three ways to think about multiplication. They are described on the back of this letter.

- **Repeated groups:** Multiplication can be used to find the total in repeated groups of the same size. In early lessons, students circle the group size in repeated-groups equations to help keep track of which factor is the group size and which is the number of groups.

4 groups of bananas

$4 \times \boxed{3} = 3 + 3 + 3 + 3 = 12$

- **Arrays:** Multiplication can be used to find the total number of items in an *array*—an arrangement of objects into rows and columns.

5 columns

2 rows   2-by-5 array

2 rows of pennies = $2 \times 5 = 10$

- **Area:** Multiplication can be used to find the area of a rectangle.

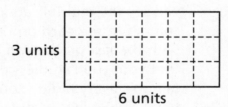

3 units

6 units

Area: 3 units × 6 units = 18 square units

Please call if you have any questions or comments.

Thank you.

Sincerely,
Your child's teacher

Multiply with 5

Estimada familia:

En esta unidad y la unidad que sigue, su niño va a practicar las multiplicaciones y divisiones básicas. *Math Expressions* incorpora en la clase el estudio, la práctica y la evaluación de las multiplicaciones y divisiones básicas. También se espera que su niño practique en casa.

Planes de estudio Todos los días su niño va a completar un plan de estudio, que indica cuáles multiplicaciones y divisiones debe estudiar esa noche. Cuando su niño haya terminado de estudiar (practicar), la persona que lo ayude debe firmar el plan de estudio.

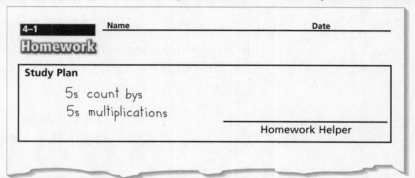

Tablas de práctica Cada vez que se presente un número nuevo, la tarea de los estudiantes incluirá una tabla de práctica. Para practicar, los estudiantes pueden cubrir los productos con un lápiz o una tira de papel grueso. Los niños dicen la multiplicación y deslizan el lápiz o el papel hacia abajo para revelar el producto después de decirlo. También pueden empezar con el último problema de la columna y deslizar el lápiz o el papel hacia arriba. Es importante que su niño practique el conteo y la multiplicación por lo menos 5 minutos cada noche. Su niño también puede usar estas tablas para practicar la división en la columna de productos desordenados cubriendo el primer factor.

	En orden	Desordenados
	1 × 5 = 5	9 × 5 = 45
	2 × 5 = 10	5 × 5 = 25
	3 × 5 = 15	2 × 5 = 10
	4 × 5 = 20	7 × 5 = 35
5	5 × 5 = 25	4 × 5 = 20
	6 × 5 = 30	6 × 5 = 30
	7 × 5 = 35	10 × 5 = 50
	8 × 5 = 40	8 × 5 = 40
	9 × 5 = 45	1 × 5 = 5
	10 × 5 = 50	3 × 5 = 15

Para ayudar a los estudiantes a comprender el concepto de la multiplicación, el programa *Math Expressions* presenta tres maneras de pensar en la multiplicación. Éstas se describen a continuación.

- **Grupos repetidos:** La multiplicación se puede usar para hallar el total con grupos del mismo tamaño que se repiten. Cuando empiezan a trabajar con ecuaciones de grupos repetidos, los estudiantes rodean con un círculo el tamaño del grupo en las ecuaciones, para recordar cuál factor representa el tamaño del grupo y cuál representa el número de grupos.

4 grupos de bananas

$4 \times ③ = 3 + 3 + 3 + 3 = 12$

- **Matrices:** Se puede usar la multiplicación para hallar el número total de objetos en una *matriz,* es decir, una disposición de objetos en filas y columnas.

5 columnas

2 filas  matriz de 2 por 5

2 filas de monedas de un centavo = $2 \times 5 = 10$

- **Área:** Se puede usar la multiplicación para hallar el área de un rectángulo.

3 unidades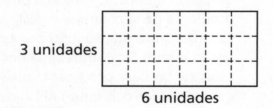

6 unidades

Área: 3 unidades × 6 unidades = 18 unidades cuadradas

Si tiene alguna duda o comentario, por favor comuníquese conmigo. Gracias.

Atentamente,
El maestro de su niño

Multiply with 5

Name _____

Date _____

Class Activity

▶Explore Repeated Groups

You can use multiplication to find the total when you have repeated groups of the same size.

$2 \times ⑤ = 5 + 5 = 10$

▶Write Multiplication Equations

Write a multiplication equation to find the total number.

1. How many bananas?

        _____

2. How many toes?

  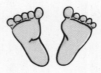   _____

3. How many wheels?

_____

►Make a Math Drawing to Solve Problems

Make a drawing for each problem. Label your drawing with a multiplication equation. Then write the answer to the problem.

Show your work.

4. Sandra bought 4 bags of lemons. There were 6 lemons in each bag. How many lemons did she buy in all?

_____

5. Batai baked 2 peach pies. He used 7 peaches per pie. How many peaches did he use in all?

_____

6. The Fuzzy Friends pet store has 3 rabbit cages. There are 5 rabbits in each cage. How many rabbits does the store have in all?

_____

7. The Paws Plus pet store has 5 rabbit cages. There are 3 rabbits in every cage. How many rabbits does the store have in all?

_____

Multiplication as Repeated Groups

Class Activity

Vocabulary

Equal Shares Drawing

▶Explore Equal Shares Drawings

Here is a problem with repeated groups. Read the problem, and think about how you would solve it.

Ms. Thomas bought 4 bags of oranges. Each bag contained 5 oranges. How many oranges did she buy in all?

You could also find the answer to this problem by making an **Equal Shares Drawing**.

Think:

⑤ ⑤ ⑤ ⑤

bags of oranges

4 × ⑤ = ☐

Equal Shares Drawing

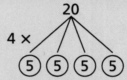

20

4 ×

⑤ ⑤ ⑤ ⑤

bags of oranges

4 × ⑤ = 20

Make an Equal Shares Drawing to solve each problem.

Show your work.

8. Ms. Gonzales bought 6 boxes of pencils. There were 5 pencils in each box. How many pencils did she buy in all?

_____

9. Mr. Franken made lunch for his 9 nieces and nephews. He put 5 carrot sticks on each of their plates. How many carrot sticks did he use in all?

_____

Name _____

Date _____

Going Further

►Function Tables

Complete each function table.

1.

Number of Tricycles	Number of Wheels
1	
2	
3	
4	
5	

2.

Number of Rabbits	Number of Ears
1	
2	
3	
4	
5	

3.

Number of Cars	Number of Wheels
1	
2	
3	
4	
5	

4.

Number of Spiders	Number of Legs
1	
2	
3	
4	
5	

Multiplication as Repeated Groups

Signature Sheet

	Count-Bys Partner	Multiplications Partner	Divisions Partner	Multiplications Sprint	Divisions Sprint
0					
1					
2					
3					
4					
5					
6					
7					
8					
9					
10					

Signature Sheet

Name _____   Date _____

Study Sheet A

5s

Count-bys	Mixed Up ×	Mixed Up ÷
1 × 5 = 5	2 × 5 = 10	10 ÷ 5 = 2
2 × 5 = 10	9 × 5 = 45	35 ÷ 5 = 7
3 × 5 = 15	1 × 5 = 5	50 ÷ 5 = 10
4 × 5 = 20	5 × 5 = 25	5 ÷ 5 = 1
5 × 5 = 25	7 × 5 = 35	20 ÷ 5 = 4
6 × 5 = 30	3 × 5 = 15	15 ÷ 5 = 3
7 × 5 = 35	10 × 5 = 50	30 ÷ 5 = 6
8 × 5 = 40	6 × 5 = 30	40 ÷ 5 = 8
9 × 5 = 45	4 × 5 = 20	25 ÷ 5 = 5
10 × 5 = 50	8 × 5 = 40	45 ÷ 5 = 9

2s

Count-bys	Mixed Up ×	Mixed Up ÷
1 × 2 = 2	7 × 2 = 14	20 ÷ 2 = 10
2 × 2 = 4	1 × 2 = 2	2 ÷ 2 = 1
3 × 2 = 6	3 × 2 = 6	6 ÷ 2 = 3
4 × 2 = 8	5 × 2 = 10	16 ÷ 2 = 8
5 × 2 = 10	6 × 2 = 12	12 ÷ 2 = 6
6 × 2 = 12	8 × 2 = 16	4 ÷ 2 = 2
7 × 2 = 14	2 × 2 = 4	10 ÷ 2 = 5
8 × 2 = 16	10 × 2 = 20	8 ÷ 2 = 4
9 × 2 = 18	4 × 2 = 8	14 ÷ 2 = 7
10 × 2 = 20	9 × 2 = 18	18 ÷ 2 = 9

10s

Count-bys	Mixed Up ×	Mixed Up ÷
1 × 10 = 10	1 × 10 = 10	80 ÷ 10 = 8
2 × 10 = 20	5 × 10 = 50	10 ÷ 10 = 1
3 × 10 = 30	2 × 10 = 20	50 ÷ 10 = 5
4 × 10 = 40	8 × 10 = 80	90 ÷ 10 = 9
5 × 10 = 50	7 × 10 = 70	40 ÷ 10 = 4
6 × 10 = 60	3 × 10 = 30	100 ÷ 10 = 10
7 × 10 = 70	4 × 10 = 40	30 ÷ 10 = 3
8 × 10 = 80	6 × 10 = 60	20 ÷ 10 = 2
9 × 10 = 90	10 × 10 = 100	70 ÷ 10 = 7
10 × 10 = 100	9 × 10 = 90	60 ÷ 10 = 6

9s

Count-bys	Mixed Up ×	Mixed Up ÷
1 × 9 = 9	2 × 9 = 18	81 ÷ 9 = 9
2 × 9 = 18	4 × 9 = 36	18 ÷ 9 = 2
3 × 9 = 27	7 × 9 = 63	36 ÷ 9 = 4
4 × 9 = 36	8 × 9 = 72	9 ÷ 9 = 1
5 × 9 = 45	3 × 9 = 27	54 ÷ 9 = 6
6 × 9 = 54	10 × 9 = 90	27 ÷ 9 = 3
7 × 9 = 63	1 × 9 = 9	63 ÷ 9 = 7
8 × 9 = 72	6 × 9 = 54	72 ÷ 9 = 8
9 × 9 = 81	5 × 9 = 45	90 ÷ 9 = 10
10 × 9 = 90	9 × 9 = 81	45 ÷ 9 = 5

UNIT 7 LESSON 3

Study Sheet A **207**

Study Sheet A

Name _____ **Date** _____

Class Activity

Vocabulary

array
row
column

► Explore Arrays

An **array** is an arrangement of objects in **rows** and **columns**. You can use multiplication to find the total number of objects in an array.

2-by-5 array
5 columns

2 rows of 5 = 2 × 5 = 10   2 rows

row

column

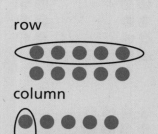

► Write Multiplication Equations

Write a multiplication equation for each array.

1. How many flowers?

_____

2. How many stamps?

_____

3. How many mugs?

_____

4. Math Journal Write a problem that you can solve by using this array. Show how to solve your problem.

Class Activity

▶ Compare Arrays

Without counting the dots in the array write >, < or = in the circle.

5.

6.

7.

8.

9.

10.

11.

12.

13. **Create Your Own** Draw two dot arrays and compare them using symbols. Then write an equation for each array to show your comparison is correct.

Multiplication and Arrays

Class Activity

►Make a Math Drawing to Solve Problems

Make a drawing for each problem. Label your drawing with a multiplication equation. Then write the answer to the problem.

Show your work.

14. The clarinet section of the band marched in 6 rows, with 2 clarinet players in each row. How many clarinet players were there in all?

_____

15. Mali put some crackers on a tray. She put the crackers in 3 rows, with 5 crackers per row. How many crackers did she put on the tray?

_____

16. Ms. Shahin set up some chairs in 7 rows, with 5 chairs in each row. How many chairs did she set up?

_____

17. Zak has a box of crayons. The crayons are arranged in 4 rows, with 6 crayons in each row. How many crayons are in the box?

_____

Vocabulary

Commutative Property of Multiplication

▶ **Explore Commutativity**

Multiplication is commutative. The **Commutative Property of Multiplication** states that you can switch the order of the factors without changing the product.

Arrays: $4 \times 5 = 5 \times 4$ **Groups:** $4 \times \text{⑤} = 5 \times \text{④}$

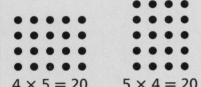

$4 \times 5 = 20$ $5 \times 4 = 20$

$4 \times \text{⑤} = 20$

$5 \times \text{④} = 20$

▶ **Solve Problems Using the Commutative Property**

Make a math drawing for each problem. Write a multiplication equation and the answer to the problem.

18. Katie bought some stickers. She put the stickers on her folder in 6 rows of 2. How many stickers did she buy?

_____

19. Marco also bought some stickers. He put the stickers on his folder in 2 rows of 6. How many stickers did he buy?

_____

20. On Monday, Juan helped Ms. Chang clean the art cabinet. He packed jars of paint in 3 boxes, with 7 jars per box. How many jars of paint did Juan put away?

_____

21. On Tuesday, Therese helped Ms. Chang. She packed jars of paint in 7 boxes, with 3 jars per box. How many jars of paint did Therese put away?

_____

Dear Family,

In addition to practice charts for the basic multiplications and divisions for each of the numbers 1 through 10, your child will bring home a variety of other practice materials over the next several weeks.

- **Home Study Sheets:** A Home Study Sheet includes 3 or 4 practice charts on one page. Your child can use the Home Study Sheets to practice all the count-bys, multiplications, and divisions for a number or to practice just the ones he or she doesn't know for that number. The Homework Helper can then use the sheet to test (or retest) your child. The Homework Helper should check with your child to see which basic multiplications or divisions he or she is ready to be tested on. The helper should mark any missed problems lightly with a pencil.

If your child gets all the answers in a column correct, the helper should sign that column on the Home Signature Sheet. When signatures are on all the columns of the Home Signature Sheet, your child should bring the sheet to school.

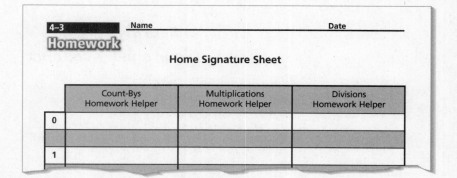

- **Home Check Sheets:** A Home Check Sheet includes columns of 20 multiplications and divisions in mixed order. These sheets can be used as a more challenging alternative to the Home Study Sheets.

- **Strategy Cards:** Students use Strategy Cards in class as flashcards, to play games, and to develop multiplication and division strategies.

Sample Multiplication Card

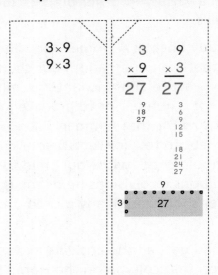

Sample Division Card

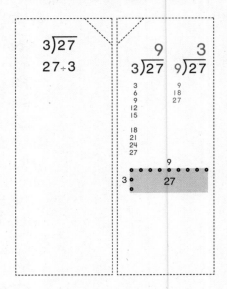

- **Games:** Near the end of this unit, students are introduced to games that provide multiplication and division practice.

Encourage your child to show you these materials and explain how they are used. Make sure your child spends time practicing multiplications and divisions every evening.

Please call if you have any questions or comments.

Thank you.

Sincerely,
Your child's teacher

Multiplication and Arrays

Estimada familia:

Además de las tablas de práctica para las multiplicaciones y divisiones básicas para cada número del 1 al 10, su niño llevará a casa una variedad de materiales de práctica en las semanas que vienen.

- **Hojas para estudiar en casa:** Una hoja para estudiar en casa incluye 3 ó 4 tablas de práctica en una página. Su niño puede usar las hojas para practicar todos los conteos, multiplicaciones y divisiones de un número, o para practicar sólo las operaciones para ese número que no domine. La persona que ayude a su niño con la tarea puede usar la hoja para hacerle una prueba (o repetir una prueba). Esa persona debe hablar con su niño para decidir sobre qué multiplicaciones o divisiones básicas el niño puede hacer la prueba. La persona que ayude debe marcar ligeramente con un lápiz cualquier problema que conteste mal. Si su niño contesta bien todas las operaciones de una columna, la persona que ayude debe firmar esa columna de la hoja de firmas. Cuando todas las columnas de la hoja de firmas estén firmadas, su niño debe llevar la hoja a la escuela.

Home Study Sheet A

5s			2s		
Count-bys	Mixed Up ×	Mixed Up ÷	Count-bys	Mixed Up ×	Mixed Up ÷
1 × 5 = 5	2 × 5 = 10	10 ÷ 5 = 2	1 × 2 = 2	7 × 2 = 14	20 ÷ 2 = 10
2 × 5 = 10	9 × 5 = 45	35 ÷ 5 = 7	2 × 2 = 4	1 × 2 = 2	2 ÷ 2 = 1
3 × 5 = 15	1 × 5 = 5	50 ÷ 5 = 10	3 × 2 = 6	3 × 2 = 6	6 ÷ 2 = 3
4 × 5 = 20	5 × 5 = 25	5 ÷ 5 = 1	4 × 2 = 8	5 × 2 = 10	16 ÷ 2 = 8
5 × 5 = 25	7 × 5 = 35	20 ÷ 5 = 4	5 × 2 = 10	6 × 2 = 12	12 ÷ 2 = 6
6 × 5 = 30	3 × 5 = 15	15 ÷ 5 = 3	6 × 2 = 12	8 × 2 = 16	4 ÷ 2 = 2
7 × 5 = 35	10 × 5 = 50	30 ÷ 5 = 6	7 × 2 = 14	2 × 2 = 4	10 ÷ 2 = 5
8 × 5 = 40	6 × 5 = 30	40 ÷ 5 = 8	8 × 2 = 16	10 × 2 = 20	8 ÷ 2 = 4
9 × 5 = 45	4 × 5 = 20	25 ÷ 5 = 5	9 × 2 = 18	4 × 2 = 8	14 ÷ 2 = 7
10 × 5 = 50	8 × 5 = 40	45 ÷ 5 = 9	10 × 2 = 20	9 × 2 = 18	18 ÷ 2 = 9

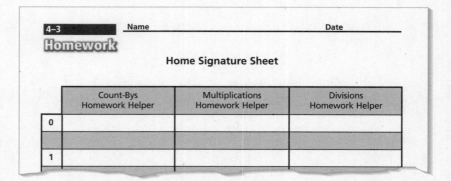

4–3

Homework

Name _____ Date _____

Home Signature Sheet

	Count-Bys Homework Helper	Multiplications Homework Helper	Divisions Homework Helper
0			
1			

- **Hojas de verificación:** Una hoja de verificación consta de columnas de 20 multiplicaciones y divisiones sin orden fijo. Estas hojas pueden usarse como alternativa de mayor desafío que las hojas para estudiar en casa.

- **Tarjetas de estrategias:** Los estudiantes usan las tarjetas de estrategias en la clase como ayuda de memoria, en juegos y para desarrollar estrategias para hacer multiplicaciones y divisións.

Ejemplo de tarjeta de multiplicación   **Ejemplo de tarjeta de división**

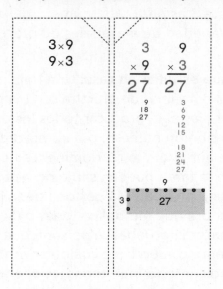
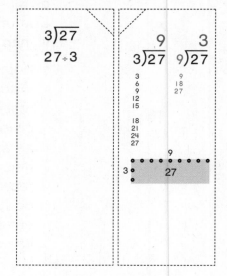

- **Juegos:** Hacia el final de esta unidad se les presentan a los estudiantes juegos para practicar la multiplicación y la división.

Anime a su niño a que le muestre a Ud. estos materiales y a que le explique cómo se usan. Asegúrese de que su niño practique la multiplicación y la división cada noche.

Si tiene alguna duda o pregunta, por favor comuníquese conmigo.

Atentamente,
El maestro de su niño

Multiplication and Arrays

Class Activity

▶ Explore Division

Solve each problem.

Vocabulary

division   divisor
dividend   quotient

1. Marc bought some bags of limes. There were
   5 limes in each bag. He bought 15 limes
   altogether. How many bags did he buy?

   _____

2. There were 10 photographs on one wall of an
   art gallery. The photographs were in rows, with
   5 photographs in each row. How many rows
   were there?

   _____

The problems above can be represented by multiplication equations
or by **division** equations.

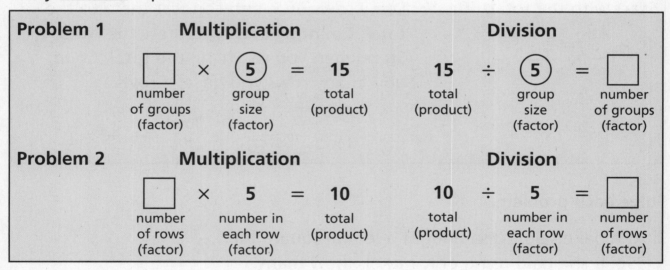

Here are ways to write a division. The following all mean
"15 divided by 5 equals 3."

$15 \div 5 = 3$ $15 / 5 = 3$ $\dfrac{15}{5} = 3$

$$\begin{array}{r} 3 \\ 5\overline{)15} \end{array}$$ ← quotient
← dividend

↑
divisor

The number you divide into is called the **dividend**. The number you
divide by is called the **divisor**. The number that is the answer to a
division problem is called the **quotient**.

Class Activity

▶ Math Tools: Equal Shares Drawings

You can use Equal Shares Drawings to help solve division problems. Here is how you might solve problem 1 on Student Activity Book page 217.

Start with the total, 15.

$15 \div \circ{5} = \square$

Draw groups of 5, and connect them to the total. Count by 5s as you draw the groups. Stop when you reach 15, the total. Count how many groups you have: 3 groups.

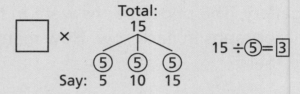

You can use a similar type of drawing to find the number of rows or columns in an array. Here is how you might solve problem 2.

Start with the total, 10.

$10 \div \circ{5} = \square$

Draw rows of 5, and connect them to the total. Count by 5s as you draw the rows. Stop when you reach 10, the total. Count how many rows you have: 2 rows.

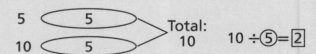

Solve each problem.

3. At a bake sale, Luisa bought a lemon square for 35¢. If she paid using only nickels, how many nickels did she spend? _____

4. Mr. Su bought a sheet of 20 stamps. There were 5 stamps in each row. How many columns of stamps were there? _____

Class Activity

▶ **Relate Division and Multiplication Equations with 5**

Find the unknown numbers.

5. 20 ÷ ⑤ = ☐   ☐ × ⑤ = 20   20 ÷ ④ = ☐   ☐ × ④ = 20

6. 10 ÷ ⑤ = ☐   ☐ × ⑤ = 10   10 ÷ ② = ☐   ☐ × ② = 10

7. 15 ÷ ⑤ = ☐   ☐ × ⑤ = 15   15 ÷ ③ = ☐   ☐ × ③ = 15

8. 40 ÷ ⑤ = ☐   ☐ × ⑤ = 40   40 ÷ ⑧ = ☐   ☐ × ⑧ = 40

9. 5 ÷ ⑤ = ☐   ☐ × ⑤ = 5   5 ÷ ① = ☐   ☐ × ① = 5

10. 25 ÷ ⑤ = ☐   ☐ × ⑤ = 25   25 ÷ ⑤ = ☐   ☐ × ⑤ = 25

11. 30 ÷ ⑤ = ☐   ☐ × ⑤ = 30   30 ÷ ⑥ = ☐   ☐ × ⑥ = 30

12. 50 ÷ ⑤ = ☐   ☐ × ⑤ = 50   50 ÷ ⑩ = ☐   ☐ × ⑩ = 50

13. 35 ÷ ⑤ = ☐   ☐ × ⑤ = 35   35 ÷ ⑦ = ☐   ☐ × ⑦ = 35

14. 45 ÷ ⑤ = ☐   ☐ × ⑤ = 45   45 ÷ ⑨ = ☐   ☐ × ⑨ = 45

▶ **Find the Number in Each Group**

Solve each problem.

15. Aziz put 15 ice cubes in 5 glasses. He put the same number of ice cubes in each glass. How many ice cubes did he put in each glass?

_____

16. Lori's uncle gave her 20 stickers. She put the same number of stickers on each of 5 folders. How many stickers did she put on each folder?

_____

17. **On the Back** Write a word problem for 30 ÷ 5 where the 5 is the size of the group. Write another word problem where 5 is the number of groups. Explain what multiplication equations the problems relate to and why.

_____

_____

_____

_____

_____

_____

_____

_____

_____

_____

_____

_____

_____

The Meaning of Division

Class Activity

Name

Date

► **Explore Patterns with 2s**

What patterns do you see below?

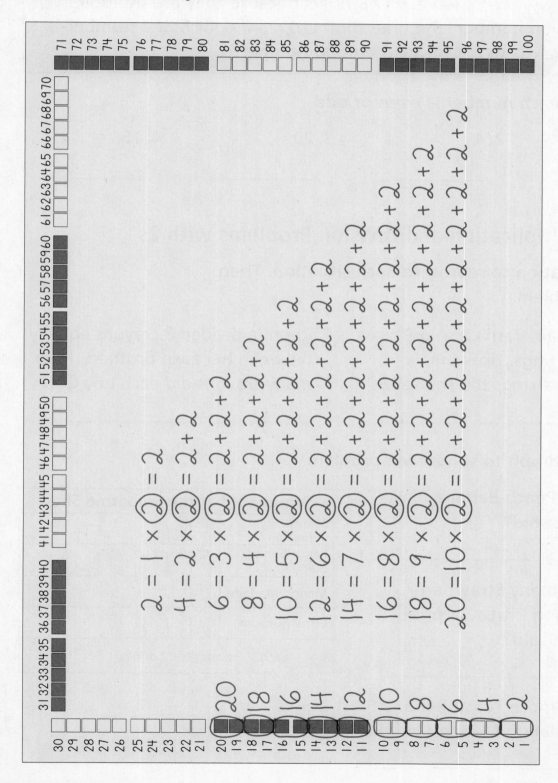

Name _____ **Date** _____

Class Activity

Vocabulary
even number
odd number

▶ Even and Odd Numbers

> The 2s count-bys are called *even numbers* because they are multiples of 2. In an **even number**, the ones digit is 0, 2, 4, 6, or 8. If a number is not a multiple of two, it is called an **odd number**.

Tell whether each number is even or odd.

1. 7

2. 4

3. 20

4. 15

_____ _____ _____ _____

▶ Solve Multiplication and Division Problems with 2s

Write an equation to represent each situation. Then solve the problem.

5. At the art fair, Tamika sold 9 pairs of earrings. How many individual earrings did she sell?

_____

6. Rhonda divided 8 crayons equally between her twin brothers. How many crayons did each boy get?

_____

Use the pictograph to solve each problem.

7. How many Peach-Banana Blast drinks were sold?

_____

8. In all, how many Strawberry Sensation and Citrus Surprise drinks were sold?

_____

Drinks Sold at the Smoothie Shop	
Strawberry Sensation	🥤🥤🥤
Peach-Banana Blast	🥤🥤🥤🥤🥤🥤🥤
Mango-Madness	🥤🥤
Citrus Surprise	🥤🥤🥤🥤🥤
Each 🥤 stands for 2 drinks.	

9. How many more Peach-Banana Blast drinks were sold than Mango Madness drinks?

_____

Multiply and Divide with 2

► **Check Sheet 1: 5s and 2s**

5s Multiplications	5s Divisions	2s Multiplications	2s Divisions
$2 \times 5 = 10$	$30 / 5 = 6$	$4 \times 2 = 8$	$8 / 2 = 4$
$5 \cdot 6 = 30$	$5 \div 5 = 1$	$2 \cdot 8 = 16$	$18 \div 2 = 9$
$5 * 9 = 45$	$15 / 5 = 3$	$1 * 2 = 2$	$2 / 2 = 1$
$4 \times 5 = 20$	$50 \div 5 = 10$	$6 \times 2 = 12$	$16 \div 2 = 8$
$5 \cdot 7 = 35$	$20 / 5 = 4$	$2 \cdot 9 = 18$	$4 / 2 = 2$
$10 * 5 = 50$	$10 \div 5 = 2$	$2 * 2 = 4$	$20 \div 2 = 10$
$1 \times 5 = 5$	$35 / 5 = 7$	$3 \times 2 = 6$	$10 / 2 = 5$
$5 \cdot 3 = 15$	$40 \div 5 = 8$	$2 \cdot 5 = 10$	$12 \div 2 = 6$
$8 * 5 = 40$	$25 / 5 = 5$	$10 * 2 = 20$	$6 / 2 = 3$
$5 \times 5 = 25$	$45 / 5 = 9$	$2 \times 7 = 14$	$14 / 2 = 7$
$5 \cdot 8 = 40$	$20 \div 5 = 4$	$2 \cdot 10 = 20$	$4 \div 2 = 2$
$7 * 5 = 35$	$15 / 5 = 3$	$9 * 2 = 18$	$2 / 2 = 1$
$5 \times 4 = 20$	$30 \div 5 = 6$	$2 \times 6 = 12$	$8 \div 2 = 4$
$6 \cdot 5 = 30$	$25 / 5 = 5$	$8 \cdot 2 = 16$	$6 / 2 = 3$
$5 * 1 = 5$	$10 \div 5 = 2$	$2 * 3 = 6$	$20 \div 2 = 10$
$5 \times 10 = 50$	$45 / 5 = 9$	$2 \times 2 = 4$	$14 / 2 = 7$
$9 \cdot 5 = 45$	$35 \div 5 = 7$	$1 \cdot 2 = 2$	$10 \div 2 = 5$
$5 * 2 = 10$	$50 \div 5 = 10$	$2 * 4 = 8$	$16 \div 2 = 8$
$3 \times 5 = 15$	$40 / 5 = 8$	$5 \times 2 = 10$	$12 / 2 = 6$
$5 \cdot 5 = 25$	$5 \div 5 = 1$	$7 \cdot 2 = 14$	$18 \div 2 = 9$

Check Sheet 1: 5s and 2s

Class Activity

Name _____

Date _____

▶ Sprints for 5s

As your teacher reads each multiplication or division, write your answer on the lines.

× 5	÷ 5
a. _____	a. _____
b. _____	b. _____
c. _____	c. _____
d. _____	d. _____
e. _____	e. _____
f. _____	f. _____
g. _____	g. _____
h. _____	h. _____
i. _____	i. _____
j. _____	j. _____

Class Activity

▶ Explore Patterns with 10s

What patterns do you see below?

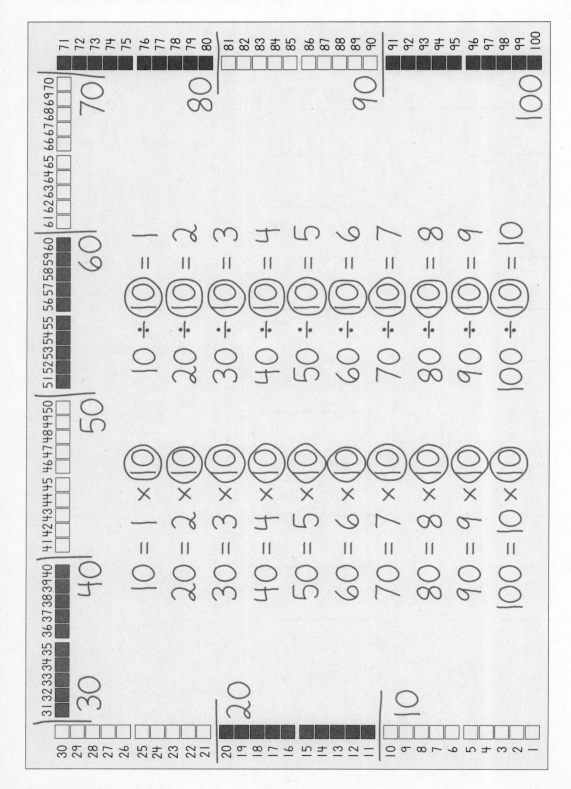

► Solve Problems with 10s

Solve each problem.

1. Raymundo has 9 dimes. How many cents does he have?

_____

2. Yoko has some dimes in her pocket, and no other coins. She has a total of 70¢. How many dimes does she have?

_____

3. Jonah picked 40 strawberries. He gave them to 10 of his friends. Each friend got the same number of strawberries. How many strawberries did each friend get?

_____

4. There are 10 Space Command trading cards in each pack. Zoe bought 5 packs of cards. How many cards did she buy in all?

_____

5. There were 80 students in the auditorium. There were 10 students in each row. How many rows of students were there?

_____

6. **On the Back** Write a word problem that can be solved using the division 60 ÷ 10. Then write a related multiplication word problem.

Multiply and Divide with 10

► **Check Sheet 2: 10s and 9s**

10s Multiplications	10s Divisions	9s Multiplications	9s Divisions
9 × 10 = 90	100 / 10 = 10	3 × 9 = 27	27 / 9 = 3
10 • 3 = 30	50 ÷ 10 = 5	9 • 7 = 63	9 ÷ 9 = 1
10 * 6 = 60	70 / 10 = 7	10 * 9 = 90	81 / 9 = 9
1 × 10 = 10	40 ÷ 10 = 4	5 × 9 = 45	45 ÷ 9 = 5
10 • 4 = 40	80 / 10 = 8	9 • 8 = 72	90 / 9 = 10
10 * 7 = 70	60 ÷ 10 = 6	9 * 1 = 9	36 ÷ 9 = 4
8 × 10 = 80	10 / 10 = 1	2 × 9 = 18	18 / 9 = 2
10 • 10 = 100	20 ÷ 10 = 2	9 • 9 = 81	63 ÷ 9 = 7
5 * 10 = 50	90 / 10 = 9	6 * 9 = 54	54 / 9 = 6
10 × 2 = 20	30 / 10 = 3	9 × 4 = 36	72 / 9 = 8
10 • 5 = 50	80 ÷ 10 = 8	9 • 5 = 45	27 ÷ 9 = 3
4 * 10 = 40	70 / 10 = 7	4 * 9 = 36	45 / 9 = 5
10 × 1 = 10	100 ÷ 10 = 10	9 × 1 = 9	63 ÷ 9 = 7
3 • 10 = 30	90 / 10 = 9	3 • 9 = 27	72 / 9 = 8
10 * 8 = 80	60 ÷ 10 = 6	9 * 8 = 72	54 ÷ 9 = 6
7 × 10 = 70	30 / 10 = 3	7 × 9 = 63	18 / 9 = 2
6 • 10 = 60	10 ÷ 10 = 1	6 • 9 = 54	90 ÷ 9 = 10
10 * 9 = 90	40 ÷ 10 = 4	9 * 9 = 81	9 ÷ 9 = 1
10 × 10 = 100	20 / 10 = 2	10 × 9 = 90	36 / 9 = 4
2 • 10 = 20	50 ÷ 10 = 5	2 • 9 = 18	81 ÷ 9 = 9

Check Sheet 2: 10s and 9s

Name _____ **Date** _____

► Explore Patterns with 9s

What patterns do you see below?

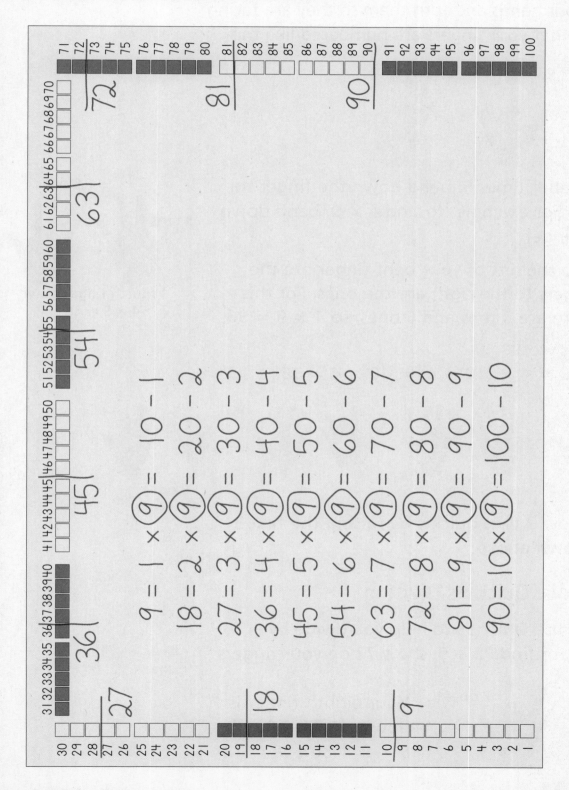

$9 = 1 \times \textcircled{9} = 10 - 1$
$18 = 2 \times \textcircled{9} = 20 - 2$
$27 = 3 \times \textcircled{9} = 30 - 3$
$36 = 4 \times \textcircled{9} = 40 - 4$
$45 = 5 \times \textcircled{9} = 50 - 5$
$54 = 6 \times \textcircled{9} = 60 - 6$
$63 = 7 \times \textcircled{9} = 70 - 7$
$72 = 8 \times \textcircled{9} = 80 - 8$
$81 = 9 \times \textcircled{9} = 90 - 9$
$90 = 10 \times \textcircled{9} = 100 - 10$

► Math Tools: Quick 9s Multiplication

You can use the Quick 9s method to help you multiply by 9. Open your hands and turn them so they are facing you. Imagine that your fingers are numbered like this.

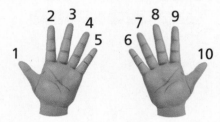

To find a number times 9, bend down the finger for that number. For example, to find 4 × 9, bend down your fourth finger.

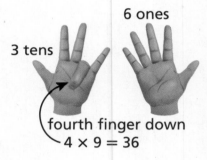

6 ones

3 tens

fourth finger down
4 × 9 = 36

The fingers to the left of your bent finger are the tens. The fingers to the right are the ones. For this problem, there are 3 tens and 6 ones, so 4 × 9 = 36.

Why does this work?
Because 4 × 9 = 4 × (10 − 1) = 40 − 4 = 36

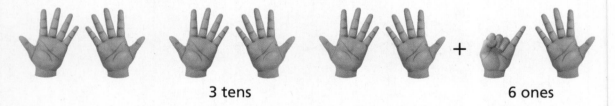

3 tens   6 ones

You could show 3 tens quickly by raising the first 3 fingers as shown above.

► Math Tools: Quick 9s Division

You can also use Quick 9s to help you divide by 9.
For example, to find 72 ÷ 9, show 72 on your fingers.

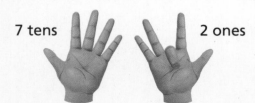

7 tens   2 ones

Your eighth finger is
down, so 72 ÷ 9 = 8.
8 × 9 = 80 − 8 = 72

Multiply and Divide with 9

Class Activity

Name _____ **Date** _____

▶ **Sprints for 2s**

As your teacher reads each multiplication or division, write your answer in the space provided.

× 2	÷ 2
a. _____	a. _____
b. _____	b. _____
c. _____	c. _____
d. _____	d. _____
e. _____	e. _____
f. _____	f. _____
g. _____	g. _____
h. _____	h. _____
i. _____	i. _____
j. _____	j. _____

▶ Check Sheet 3: 2s, 5s, 9s, and 10s

2s, 5s, 9s, 10s Multiplications	2s, 5s, 9s, 10s Multiplications	2s, 5s, 9s, 10s Divisions	2s, 5s, 9s, 10s Divisions
$2 \times 10 = 20$	$5 \times 10 = 50$	$18 / 2 = 9$	$36 / 9 = 4$
$10 \cdot 5 = 50$	$10 \cdot 9 = 90$	$50 \div 5 = 10$	$70 \div 10 = 7$
$9 * 6 = 54$	$4 * 10 = 40$	$72 / 9 = 8$	$18 / 2 = 9$
$7 \times 10 = 70$	$2 \times 9 = 18$	$60 \div 10 = 6$	$45 \div 5 = 9$
$2 \cdot 3 = 6$	$5 \cdot 3 = 15$	$12 / 2 = 6$	$45 / 9 = 5$
$5 * 7 = 35$	$6 * 9 = 54$	$30 \div 5 = 6$	$30 \div 10 = 3$
$9 \times 10 = 90$	$10 \times 3 = 30$	$18 / 9 = 2$	$6 / 2 = 3$
$6 \cdot 10 = 60$	$3 \cdot 2 = 6$	$50 \div 10 = 5$	$50 \div 5 = 10$
$8 * 2 = 16$	$5 * 8 = 40$	$14 / 2 = 7$	$27 / 9 = 3$
$5 \times 6 = 30$	$9 \times 9 = 81$	$25 / 5 = 5$	$70 / 10 = 7$
$9 \cdot 5 = 45$	$10 \cdot 4 = 40$	$81 \div 9 = 9$	$20 \div 2 = 10$
$8 * 10 = 80$	$9 * 2 = 18$	$20 / 10 = 2$	$45 / 5 = 9$
$2 \times 1 = 2$	$5 \times 1 = 5$	$8 \div 2 = 4$	$54 \div 9 = 6$
$3 \cdot 5 = 15$	$9 \cdot 6 = 54$	$45 / 5 = 9$	$80 / 10 = 8$
$4 * 9 = 36$	$10 * 1 = 10$	$63 \div 9 = 7$	$16 \div 2 = 8$
$3 \times 10 = 30$	$7 \times 2 = 14$	$30 / 10 = 3$	$15 / 5 = 3$
$2 \cdot 6 = 12$	$6 \cdot 5 = 30$	$10 \div 2 = 5$	$90 \div 9 = 10$
$4 * 5 = 20$	$8 * 9 = 72$	$40 \div 5 = 8$	$100 \div 10 = 10$
$9 \times 7 = 63$	$10 \times 6 = 60$	$9 / 9 = 1$	$12 / 2 = 6$
$1 \cdot 10 = 10$	$2 \cdot 8 = 16$	$50 \div 10 = 5$	$35 \div 5 = 7$

Check Sheet 3: 2s, 5s, 9s, and 10s

▶ **Solve Word Problems with 2s, 5s, 9s, and 10s**

Write an equation to represent each problem. Then solve the problem.

1. Ian planted tulip bulbs in an array with 5 rows and 10 columns. How many bulbs did he plant?

_____

2. Erin gave 30 basketball cards to her 5 cousins. Each cousin got the same number of cards. How many cards did each cousin get?

_____

3. Martina bought 7 cans of racquetballs. There were 2 balls per can. How many racquetballs did she buy in all?

_____

4. The 27 students in the orchestra stood in rows for their school picture. There were 9 students in every row. How many rows of students were there?

_____

► Math Tools: Fast-Array Drawings

When you solve a word problem involving an array, you can save time by making a Fast-Array drawing. This type of drawing shows the number of items in each row and column, but does not show every single item.

Here is how you might use a Fast-Array drawing for problem 1 on Student Activity Book page 235.

Show the number of rows and the number of columns. Make a box in the center to show that you don't know the total.

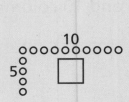

Here are three ways to find the total.

• Find 5×10.

• Use 10s count-bys to find the total in 5 rows of 10: 10, 20, 30, 40, 50.

• Use 5s count-bys to find the total in 10 rows of 5: 5, 10, 15, 20, 25, 30, 35, 40, 45, 50.

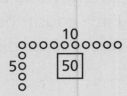

Here is how you might use a Fast-Array drawing for problem 4.

Show the number in each row and the total. Make a box to show that you don't know the number of rows.

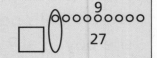

Here are two ways to find the number of rows.

• Find $27 \div 9$ or solve $\boxed{} \times 9 = 27$.

• Count by 9s until you reach 27: 9, 18, 27.

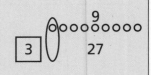

➡ **Math Journal** **Make a Fast-Array Drawing to solve each problem.**

5. Beth planted tulip bulbs in an array with 9 rows and 6 columns. How many bulbs did she plant?

6. The 36 students in the chorus stood in 4 rows for their school picture. How many students were in each row?

Class Activity

Name _____

Date _____

► **Sprints for 10s**

As your teacher reads each multiplication or division, write your answer in the space provided.

× 10	÷ 10
a. _____	a. _____
b. _____	b. _____
c. _____	c. _____
d. _____	d. _____
e. _____	e. _____
f. _____	f. _____
g. _____	g. _____
h. _____	h. _____
i. _____	i. _____
j. _____	j. _____

Class Activity

► **Explore Patterns with 3s**

What patterns do you see below?

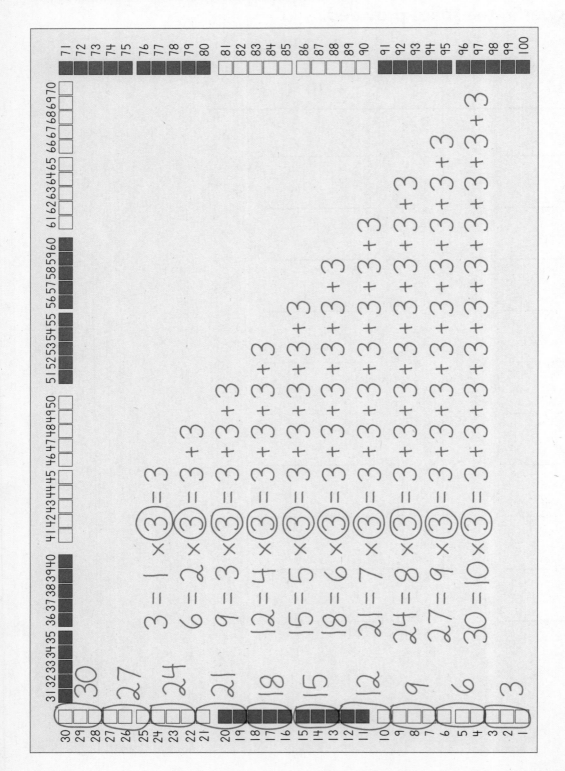

Multiply and Divide with 3

Class Activity

▶ Use the 5s Shortcut for 3s

Write the 3s count-bys to find the total.

1. How many sides are in 8 triangles?

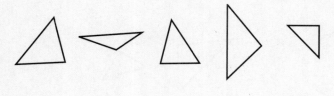 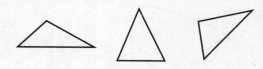

___ ___ ___ ___ ___   ___ ___ ___

2. How many wheels are on 6 tricycles?

___ ___ ___ ___ ___   ___

3. How many legs are on 7 tripods?

___ ___ ___ ___ ___   ___ ___

Class Activity

Find the total by starting with the fifth count-by and counting by 3s from there.

4. How many sides are in 7 triangles?

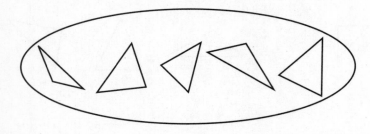 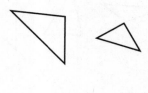

_____   _____

5. How many wheels are on 9 tricycles?

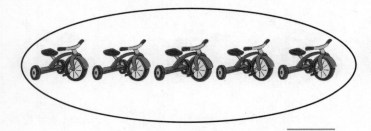 

_____   ___ ___ ___ ___

6. How many legs are on 8 tripods?

_____   ___ ___ ___

Multiply and Divide with 3

Name _____ **Date** _____

Going Further

►Represent Numbers in Different Ways

You can represent numbers in different ways. Here are some equivalent expressions for 9.

3×3	$81 \div 9$	$5 + 4$	$19 - 10$	$2 \times 3 + 3$
$5 + 3 + 1$	9×1	$18 - 9$	$63 \div 7$	$3 + 6$
$20 - 11$	$4 \times 2 + 1$	$54 \div 6$	$9 + 0$	$14 - 5$

Circle the expression which does not represent the number given.

1. 8

2×4 $\qquad$ $5 + 4$ $\qquad$ $72 \div 9$

2. 10

2×5 $\qquad$ $40 \div 4$ $\qquad$ $28 - 17$

3. 18

2×8 $\qquad$ $28 - 10$ $\qquad$ $9 + 9$

4. 30

6×5 $\qquad$ $50 - 20$ $\qquad$ $15 + 16$

5. 35

8×5 $\qquad$ $29 + 6$ $\qquad$ $40 - 5$

6. 40

10×4 $\qquad$ 8×5 $\qquad$ $20 + 21$

7. 54

$51 + 3$ $\qquad$ 9×6 $\qquad$ $56 - 3$

8. 72

9×7 $\qquad$ $69 + 3$ $\qquad$ 9×8

Write 3 equivalent expressions for each number.

9. 2

_____

_____

_____

10. 3

_____

_____

_____

11. 5

_____

_____

_____

12. 24

_____

_____

_____

13. 36

_____

_____

_____

14. 50

_____

_____

_____

15. 63

_____

_____

_____

16. 100

_____

_____

_____

Multiply and Divide with 3

Study Sheet B

4s

Count-bys	Mixed Up ×	Mixed Up ÷
1 × 4 = 4	4 × 4 = 16	12 ÷ 4 = 3
2 × 4 = 8	1 × 4 = 4	36 ÷ 4 = 9
3 × 4 = 12	7 × 4 = 28	24 ÷ 4 = 6
4 × 4 = 16	3 × 4 = 12	4 ÷ 4 = 1
5 × 4 = 20	9 × 4 = 36	20 ÷ 4 = 5
6 × 4 = 24	10 × 4 = 40	28 ÷ 4 = 7
7 × 4 = 28	2 × 4 = 8	8 ÷ 4 = 2
8 × 4 = 32	5 × 4 = 20	40 ÷ 4 = 10
9 × 4 = 36	8 × 4 = 32	32 ÷ 4 = 8
10 × 4 = 40	6 × 4 = 24	16 ÷ 4 = 4

1s

Count-bys	Mixed Up ×	Mixed Up ÷
1 × 1 = 1	5 × 1 = 5	10 ÷ 1 = 10
2 × 1 = 2	7 × 1 = 7	8 ÷ 1 = 8
3 × 1 = 3	10 × 1 = 10	4 ÷ 1 = 4
4 × 1 = 4	1 × 1 = 1	9 ÷ 1 = 9
5 × 1 = 5	8 × 1 = 8	6 ÷ 1 = 6
6 × 1 = 6	4 × 1 = 4	7 ÷ 1 = 7
7 × 1 = 7	9 × 1 = 9	1 ÷ 1 = 1
8 × 1 = 8	3 × 1 = 3	2 ÷ 1 = 2
9 × 1 = 9	2 × 1 = 2	5 ÷ 1 = 5
10 × 1 = 10	6 × 1 = 6	3 ÷ 1 = 3

3s

Count-bys	Mixed Up ×	Mixed Up ÷
1 × 3 = 3	5 × 3 = 15	27 ÷ 3 = 9
2 × 3 = 6	1 × 3 = 3	6 ÷ 3 = 2
3 × 3 = 9	8 × 3 = 24	18 ÷ 3 = 6
4 × 3 = 12	10 × 3 = 30	30 ÷ 3 = 10
5 × 3 = 15	3 × 3 = 9	9 ÷ 3 = 3
6 × 3 = 18	7 × 3 = 21	3 ÷ 3 = 1
7 × 3 = 21	9 × 3 = 27	12 ÷ 3 = 4
8 × 3 = 24	2 × 3 = 6	24 ÷ 3 = 8
9 × 3 = 27	4 × 3 = 12	15 ÷ 3 = 5
10 × 3 = 30	6 × 3 = 18	21 ÷ 3 = 7

0s

Count-bys	Mixed Up ×
1 × 0 = 0	3 × 0 = 0
2 × 0 = 0	10 × 0 = 0
3 × 0 = 0	5 × 0 = 0
4 × 0 = 0	8 × 0 = 0
5 × 0 = 0	7 × 0 = 0
6 × 0 = 0	2 × 0 = 0
7 × 0 = 0	9 × 0 = 0
8 × 0 = 0	6 × 0 = 0
9 × 0 = 0	1 × 0 = 0
10 × 0 = 0	4 × 0 = 0

Study Sheet B

2×2

$\begin{array}{r} 2 \\ \times 3 \end{array}$ $\begin{array}{r} 3 \\ \times 2 \end{array}$

2×4
4×2

$\begin{array}{r} 2 \\ \times 5 \end{array}$ $\begin{array}{r} 5 \\ \times 2 \end{array}$

2×6
6×2

$\begin{array}{r} 2 \\ \times 7 \end{array}$ $\begin{array}{r} 7 \\ \times 2 \end{array}$

2×8
8×2

$\begin{array}{r} 2 \\ \times 9 \end{array}$ $\begin{array}{r} 9 \\ \times 2 \end{array}$

$10 = 2 \times 5$

$10 = 5 \times 2$

5   2
10   4
      6
      8
     10

5
2 ○○○○○
  ○ 10

$\begin{array}{r} 2 \\ \times 4 \\ \hline 8 \end{array}$
$\begin{array}{r} 4 \\ \times 2 \\ \hline 8 \end{array}$

2   4
4   8
6
8

2
○○
4 ○ 8
○
○

$6 = 2 \times 3$

$6 = 3 \times 2$

3   2
6   4
      6

3
2 ○○○
  ○ 6

$\begin{array}{r} 2 \\ \times 2 \\ \hline 4 \end{array}$

2
4

2
○○
2 ○ 4

$18 = 2 \times 9$

$18 = 9 \times 2$

9   2
18   4
     6
     8
   10

   12
   14
   16
   18

9
2 ○○○○○○○○○
  ○ 18

$\begin{array}{r} 2 \\ \times 8 \\ \hline 16 \end{array}$
$\begin{array}{r} 8 \\ \times 2 \\ \hline 16 \end{array}$

8   2
16   4
     6
     8
   10

   12
   14
   16

2
○
○
○
○
8 ○ 16
○
○
○

$14 = 2 \times 7$

$14 = 7 \times 2$

7   2
14   4
   6
   8
  10

  12
  14

7
2 ○○○○○○○
  ○ 14

$\begin{array}{r} 2 \\ \times 6 \\ \hline 12 \end{array}$
$\begin{array}{r} 6 \\ \times 2 \\ \hline 12 \end{array}$

6   2
12   4
   6
   8
  10

  12

2
○
○
○
6 ○ 12
○
○

Multiplication Strategy Cards

3×3

$$\begin{array}{r} 3 \\ \times\,4 \\ \hline \end{array} \qquad \begin{array}{r} 4 \\ \times\,3 \\ \hline \end{array}$$

3×5
5×3

$$\begin{array}{r} 3 \\ \times\,6 \\ \hline \end{array} \qquad \begin{array}{r} 6 \\ \times\,3 \\ \hline \end{array}$$

3×7
7×3

$$\begin{array}{r} 3 \\ \times\,8 \\ \hline \end{array} \qquad \begin{array}{r} 8 \\ \times\,3 \\ \hline \end{array}$$

3×9
9×3

$$\begin{array}{r} 4 \\ \times\,4 \\ \hline \end{array}$$

Card 1:

$18 = 3 \times 6$

$18 = 6 \times 3$

6	3
12	6
18	9
	12
	15
	18

6
3 · 18

Card 2:

$\begin{array}{r} 3 \\ \times 5 \\ \hline 15 \end{array}$ $\begin{array}{r} 5 \\ \times 3 \\ \hline 15 \end{array}$

5	3
10	6
15	9
	12
	15

3
5 · 15

Card 3:

$12 = 3 \times 4$

$12 = 4 \times 3$

4	3
8	6
12	9
	12

4
3 · 12

Card 4:

$\begin{array}{r} 3 \\ \times 3 \\ \hline 9 \end{array}$

3
6
9

3
3 · 9

Card 5:

$16 = 4 \times 4$

4
8
12
16

4
4 · 16

Card 6:

$\begin{array}{r} 3 \\ \times 9 \\ \hline 27 \end{array}$ $\begin{array}{r} 9 \\ \times 3 \\ \hline 27 \end{array}$

9	3
18	6
27	9
	12
	15
	18
	21
	24
	27

9
3 · 27

Card 7:

$24 = 3 \times 8$

$24 = 8 \times 3$

8	3
16	6
24	9
	12
	15
	18
	21
	24

3
8 · 24

Card 8:

$\begin{array}{r} 3 \\ \times 7 \\ \hline 21 \end{array}$ $\begin{array}{r} 7 \\ \times 3 \\ \hline 21 \end{array}$

7	3
14	6
21	9
	12
	15
	18
	21

7
3 · 21

Multiplication Strategy Cards

4 × 5
5 × 4

4   6
× 6   × 4

4 × 7
7 × 4

4   8
× 8   × 4

4 × 9
9 × 4

5
× 5

5 × 6
6 × 5

5   7
× 7   × 5

Card 1
$$32 = 4 \times 8$$
$$32 = 8 \times 4$$

8	4
16	8
24	12
32	16
	20
	24
	28
	32

4

8 | 32

Card 2

4	7
$\times 7$	$\times 4$
28	**28**

7	4
14	8
21	12
28	16
	20
	24
	28

7

4 | 28

Card 3
$$24 = 4 \times 6$$
$$24 = 6 \times 4$$

6	4
12	8
18	12
24	16
	20
	24

4

6 | 24

Card 4

4	5
$\times 5$	$\times 4$
20	**20**

5	4
10	8
15	12
20	16
	20

5

4 | 20

Card 5
$$35 = 5 \times 7$$
$$35 = 7 \times 5$$

7	5
14	10
21	15
28	20
35	25
	30
	35

7

5 | 35

Card 6

5	6
$\times 6$	$\times 5$
30	**30**

6	5
12	10
18	15
24	20
30	25
	30

5

6 | 30

Card 7
$$25 = 5 \times 5$$

5
10
15
20
25

5

5 | 25

Card 8

4	9
$\times 9$	$\times 4$
36	**36**

9	4
18	8
27	12
36	16
	20
	24
	28
	32
	36

9

4 | 36

Multiplication Strategy Cards

5×8
8×5

$\begin{array}{r} 5 \\ \times 9 \\ \hline \end{array}$ $\begin{array}{r} 9 \\ \times 5 \\ \hline \end{array}$

6×6

$\begin{array}{r} 6 \\ \times 7 \\ \hline \end{array}$ $\begin{array}{r} 7 \\ \times 6 \\ \hline \end{array}$

6×8
8×6

$\begin{array}{r} 6 \\ \times 9 \\ \hline \end{array}$ $\begin{array}{r} 9 \\ \times 6 \\ \hline \end{array}$

7×7

$\begin{array}{r} 7 \\ \times 8 \\ \hline \end{array}$ $\begin{array}{r} 8 \\ \times 7 \\ \hline \end{array}$

Card 1

$42 = 7 \times 6$

$42 = 6 \times 7$

6	7
12	14
18	21
24	28
30	35
36	42
42	

7

6 | 42

Card 2

6
$\times 6$
36

6
12
18
24
30
36

6

6 | 36

Card 3

$45 = 9 \times 5$

$45 = 5 \times 9$

5	9
10	18
15	27
20	36
25	45
30	
35	
40	
45	

9

5 | 45

Card 4

8 $\times 5$ 40 5 $\times 8$ 40

5	8
10	16
15	24
20	32
25	40
30	
35	
40	

5

8 | 40

Card 5

$56 = 7 \times 8$

$56 = 8 \times 7$

8	7
16	14
24	21
32	28
40	35
48	42
56	49
	56

8

7 | 56

Card 6

7
$\times 7$
49

7
14
21
28
35
42
49

7

7 | 49

Card 7

$54 = 9 \times 6$

$54 = 6 \times 9$

6	9
12	18
18	27
24	36
30	45
36	54
42	
48	
54	

9

6 | 54

Card 8

6 $\times 8$ 48 8 $\times 6$ 48

6	8
12	16
18	24
24	32
30	40
36	48
42	
48	

8

6 | 48

Multiplication Strategy Cards

7×9
9×7

8
$\times\ 8$

9×8
8×9

9
$\times\ 9$

Card 1

$81 = 9 \times 9$

9
18
27
36
45

54
63
72
81

[array diagram: 9 by 9 = 81]

Card 2

$$\begin{array}{r} 9 \\ \times\ 8 \\ \hline 72 \end{array} \qquad \begin{array}{r} 8 \\ \times\ 9 \\ \hline 72 \end{array}$$

8   9
16   18
24   27
32   36
40   45

48   54
56   63
64   72
72

[array diagram: 9 by 8 = 72]

Card 3

$64 = 8 \times 8$

8
16
24
32
40

48
56
64

[array diagram: 8 by 8 = 64]

Card 4

$$\begin{array}{r} 7 \\ \times\ 9 \\ \hline 63 \end{array} \qquad \begin{array}{r} 9 \\ \times\ 7 \\ \hline 63 \end{array}$$

9   7
18   14
27   21
36   28
45   35

54   42
63   49
         56
         63

[array diagram: 9 by 7 = 63]

Multiplication Strategy Cards

$2\overline{)4}$

$4 \div 2$

$2\overline{)6}$

$6 \div 2$

$2\overline{)8}$

$8 \div 2$

$2\overline{)10}$

$10 \div 2$

$2\overline{)12}$

$12 \div 2$

$2\overline{)14}$

$14 \div 2$

$2\overline{)16}$

$16 \div 2$

$2\overline{)18}$

$18 \div 2$

Division Strategy Cards — Unit 7 Lesson 10

Card 1

$$2\overline{)10}\;\;5 \qquad 5\overline{)10}\;\;2$$

2
4
6
8
10

5 · · · · · | 2 · · | 10

Card 2

$$2\overline{)8}\;\;4 \qquad 4\overline{)8}\;\;2$$

2
4
6
8

4 · · · · | 2 · · | 8

Card 3

$$2\overline{)6}\;\;3 \qquad 3\overline{)6}\;\;2$$

2
4
6

3 · · · | 2 · · | 6

Card 4

$$2\overline{)4}\;\;2$$

2
4

2 · · | 2 · · | 4

Card 5

$$2\overline{)18}\;\;9 \qquad 9\overline{)18}\;\;2$$

2
4
6
8
10

12
14
16
18

9 · · · · · · · · · | 2 · · | 18

Card 6

$$2\overline{)16}\;\;8 \qquad 8\overline{)16}\;\;2$$

2
4
6
8
10

12
14
16

8 · · · · · · · · | 2 · · | 16

Card 7

$$2\overline{)14}\;\;7 \qquad 7\overline{)14}\;\;2$$

2
4
6
8
10

12
14

7 · · · · · · · | 2 · · | 14

Card 8

$$2\overline{)12}\;\;6 \qquad 6\overline{)12}\;\;2$$

2
4
6
8
10

12

6 · · · · · · | 2 · · | 12

Division Strategy Cards

$3\overline{)6}$

$6 \div 3$

$4\overline{)8}$

$8 \div 4$

$5\overline{)10}$

$10 \div 5$

$6\overline{)12}$

$12 \div 6$

$7\overline{)14}$

$14 \div 7$

$8\overline{)16}$

$16 \div 8$

$9\overline{)18}$

$18 \div 9$

$3\overline{)9}$

$9 \div 3$

2
$6 \overline{)12}$

6
12

6
$2 \overline{)12}$

2
4
6
8
10

12

2

6 ∘ 12

2
$5 \overline{)10}$

5
10

5
$2 \overline{)10}$

2
4
6
8
10

2

5 ∘ 10

2
$4 \overline{)8}$

4
8

4
$2 \overline{)8}$

2
4
6
8

2

4 ∘ 8

2
$3 \overline{)6}$

3
6

3
$2 \overline{)6}$

2
4
6

2

3 ∘ 6

3
$3 \overline{)9}$

3
6
9

3

3 ∘ 9

2
$9 \overline{)18}$

9
18

9
$2 \overline{)18}$

2
4
6
8
10

12
14
16
18

2

9 ∘ 18

2
$8 \overline{)16}$

8
16

8
$2 \overline{)16}$

2
4
6
8
10

12
14
16

2

8 ∘ 16

2
$7 \overline{)14}$

7
14

7
$2 \overline{)14}$

2
4
6
8
10

12
14

2

7 ∘ 14

Division Strategy Cards

$3\overline{)12}$

$12 \div 3$

$3\overline{)15}$

$15 \div 3$

$3\overline{)18}$

$18 \div 3$

$3\overline{)21}$

$21 \div 3$

$3\overline{)24}$

$24 \div 3$

$3\overline{)27}$

$27 \div 3$

$4\overline{)12}$

$12 \div 4$

$5\overline{)15}$

$15 \div 5$

Card 1

$$7 \atop 3\overline{)21}$$ $$3 \atop 7\overline{)21}$$

3	7
6	14
9	21
12	
15	
18	
21	

7
3 | 21

Card 2

$$6 \atop 3\overline{)18}$$ $$3 \atop 6\overline{)18}$$

3	6
6	12
9	18
12	
15	
18	

6
3 | 18

Card 3

$$5 \atop 3\overline{)15}$$ $$3 \atop 5\overline{)15}$$

3	5
6	10
9	15
12	
15	

5
3 | 15

Card 4

$$4 \atop 3\overline{)12}$$ $$3 \atop 4\overline{)12}$$

3	4
6	8
9	12
12	

4
3 | 12

Card 5

$$3 \atop 5\overline{)15}$$ $$5 \atop 3\overline{)15}$$

5	3
10	6
15	9
	12
	15

3
5 | 15

Card 6

$$3 \atop 4\overline{)12}$$ $$4 \atop 3\overline{)12}$$

4	3
8	6
12	9
	12

3
4 | 12

Card 7

$$9 \atop 3\overline{)27}$$ $$3 \atop 9\overline{)27}$$

3	9
6	18
9	27
12	
15	
18	
21	
24	
27	

9
3 | 27

Card 8

$$8 \atop 3\overline{)24}$$ $$3 \atop 8\overline{)24}$$

3	8
6	16
9	24
12	
15	
18	
21	
24	

8
3 | 24

Division Strategy Cards

$6 \overline{)18}$	$7 \overline{)21}$	$8 \overline{)24}$	$9 \overline{)27}$
$18 \div 6$	$21 \div 7$	$24 \div 8$	$27 \div 9$

$4 \overline{)16}$	$4 \overline{)20}$	$4 \overline{)24}$	$4 \overline{)28}$
$16 \div 4$	$20 \div 4$	$24 \div 4$	$28 \div 4$

Division Strategy Cards

Card 1

$$3 \overline{)9 \overline{)27}} \qquad 9 \overline{)3 \overline{)27}}$$

9	3
18	6
27	9
	12
	15
	18
	21
	24
	27

3

9 ○ 27

Card 2

$$3 \overline{)8 \overline{)24}} \qquad 8 \overline{)3 \overline{)24}}$$

8	3
16	6
24	9
	12
	15
	18
	21
	24

3

8 ○ 24

Card 3

$$3 \overline{)7 \overline{)21}} \qquad 7 \overline{)3 \overline{)21}}$$

7	3
14	6
21	9
	12
	15
	18
	21

3

7 ○ 21

Card 4

$$3 \overline{)6 \overline{)18}} \qquad 6 \overline{)3 \overline{)18}}$$

6	3
12	6
18	9
	12
	15
	18

3

6 ○ 18

Card 5

$$7 \overline{)4 \overline{)28}} \qquad 4 \overline{)7 \overline{)28}}$$

4	7
8	14
12	21
16	28
20	
24	
28	

7

4 28

Card 6

$$6 \overline{)4 \overline{)24}} \qquad 4 \overline{)6 \overline{)24}}$$

4	6
8	12
12	18
16	24
20	
24	

6

4 24

Card 7

$$5 \overline{)4 \overline{)20}} \qquad 4 \overline{)5 \overline{)20}}$$

4	5
8	10
12	15
16	20
20	

5

4 20

Card 8

$$4 \overline{)4 \overline{)16}}$$

4
8
12
16

4

4 16

Division Strategy Cards

$4\overline{)32}$

$32 \div 4$

$4\overline{)36}$

$36 \div 4$

$5\overline{)20}$

$20 \div 5$

$6\overline{)24}$

$24 \div 6$

$7\overline{)28}$

$28 \div 7$

$8\overline{)32}$

$32 \div 8$

$9\overline{)36}$

$36 \div 9$

$5\overline{)25}$

$25 \div 5$

Division Strategy Cards

Card 1
4   6)24   4)24

6, 12, 18, 24   4, 8, 12, 16, 20, 24

4 — 6 — 24

Card 2
4   5)20   4)20

5, 10, 15, 20   4, 8, 12, 16, 20

4 — 5 — 20

Card 3
9   4)36   4   9)36

4, 8, 12, 16, 20, 24, 28, 32, 36   9, 18, 27, 36

9 — 4 — 36

Card 4
8   4)32   4   8)32

4, 8, 12, 16, 20, 24, 28, 32   8, 16, 24, 32

8 — 4 — 32

Card 5
5   5)25

5, 10, 15, 20, 25

5 — 5 — 25

Card 6
4   9)36   9   4)36

9, 18, 27, 36   4, 8, 12, 16, 20, 24, 28, 32, 36

4 — 9 — 36

Card 7
4   8)32   8   4)32

8, 16, 24, 32   4, 8, 12, 16, 20, 24, 28, 32

4 — 8 — 32

Card 8
4   7)28   7   4)28

7, 14, 21, 28   4, 8, 12, 16, 20, 24, 28

4 — 7 — 28

Division Strategy Cards

$5\overline{)30}$

$30 \div 5$

$5\overline{)35}$

$35 \div 5$

$5\overline{)40}$

$40 \div 5$

$5\overline{)45}$

$45 \div 5$

$6\overline{)30}$

$30 \div 6$

$7\overline{)35}$

$35 \div 7$

$8\overline{)40}$

$40 \div 8$

$9\overline{)45}$

$45 \div 9$

$\begin{array}{r}9\\5\overline{)45}\end{array}$ $\begin{array}{r}5\\9\overline{)45}\end{array}$

5	9
10	18
15	27
20	36
25	45
30	
35	
40	
45	

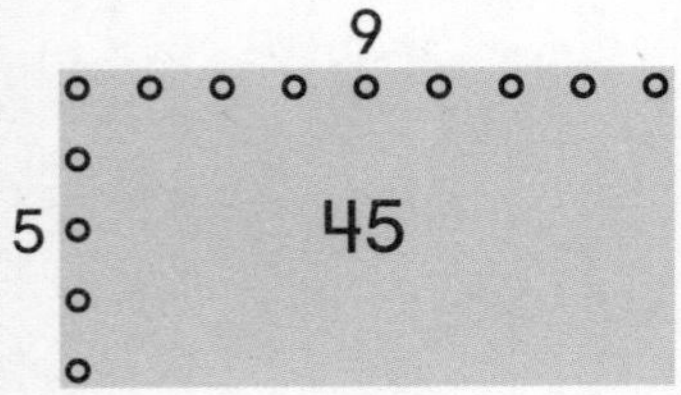

$\begin{array}{r}8\\5\overline{)40}\end{array}$ $\begin{array}{r}5\\8\overline{)40}\end{array}$

5	8
10	16
15	24
20	32
25	40
30	
35	
40	

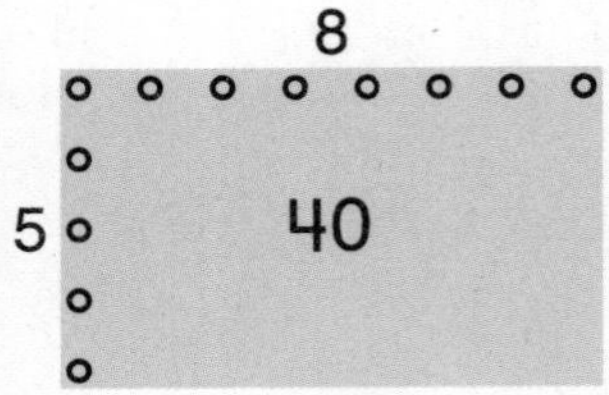

$\begin{array}{r}7\\5\overline{)35}\end{array}$ $\begin{array}{r}5\\7\overline{)35}\end{array}$

5	7
10	14
15	21
20	28
25	35
30	
35	

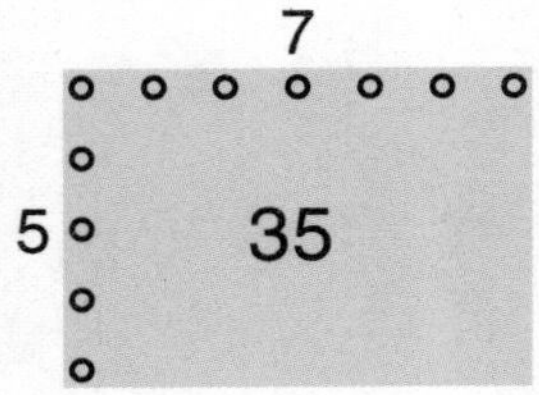

$\begin{array}{r}6\\5\overline{)30}\end{array}$ $\begin{array}{r}5\\6\overline{)30}\end{array}$

5	6
10	12
15	18
20	24
25	30
30	

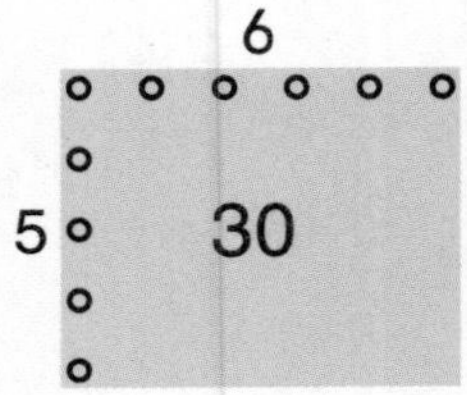

$\begin{array}{r}5\\9\overline{)45}\end{array}$ $\begin{array}{r}9\\5\overline{)45}\end{array}$

9	5
18	10
27	15
36	20
45	25
	30
	35
	40
	45

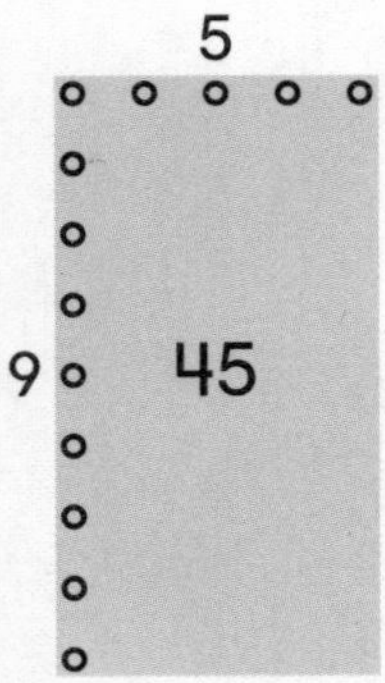

$\begin{array}{r}5\\8\overline{)40}\end{array}$ $\begin{array}{r}8\\5\overline{)40}\end{array}$

8	5
16	10
24	15
32	20
40	25
	30
	35
	40

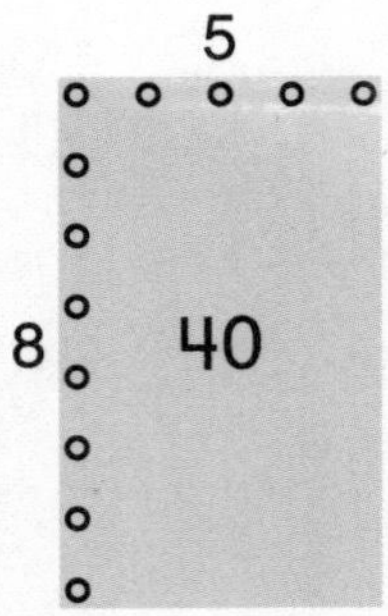

$\begin{array}{r}5\\7\overline{)35}\end{array}$ $\begin{array}{r}7\\5\overline{)35}\end{array}$

7	5
14	10
21	15
28	20
35	25
	30
	35

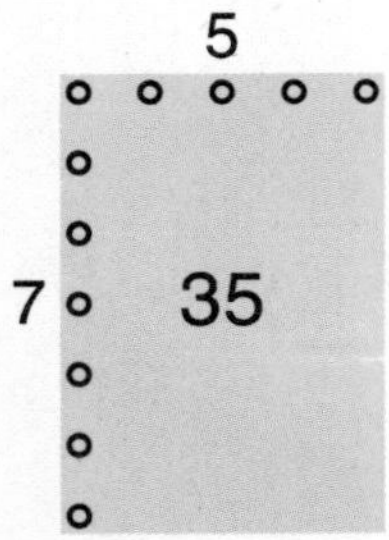

$\begin{array}{r}5\\6\overline{)30}\end{array}$ $\begin{array}{r}6\\5\overline{)30}\end{array}$

6	5
12	10
18	15
24	20
30	25
	30

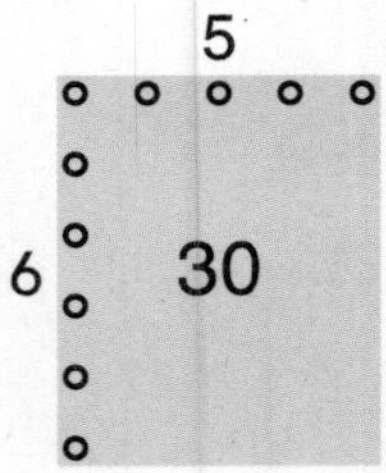

$6\overline{)36}$
$36 \div 6$

$6\overline{)42}$
$42 \div 6$

$6\overline{)48}$
$48 \div 6$

$6\overline{)54}$
$54 \div 6$

$7\overline{)42}$
$42 \div 7$

$8\overline{)48}$
$48 \div 8$

$9\overline{)54}$
$54 \div 9$

$7\overline{)49}$
$49 \div 7$

9 6
$6\overline{)54}$ $9\overline{)54}$

6	9
12	18
18	27
24	36
30	45
36	54
42	
48	
54	

9
6 54

8 6
$6\overline{)48}$ $8\overline{)48}$

6	8
12	16
18	24
24	32
30	40
36	48
42	
48	

8
6 48

7 6
$6\overline{)42}$ $7\overline{)42}$

6	7
12	14
18	21
24	28
30	35
36	42
42	

7
6 42

6
$6\overline{)36}$

| 6 |
| 12 |
| 18 |
| 24 |
| 30 |
| |
| 36 |

6
6 36

7
$7\overline{)49}$

| 7 |
| 14 |
| 21 |
| 28 |
| 35 |
| |
| 42 |
| 49 |

7
7 49

6 9
$9\overline{)54}$ $6\overline{)54}$

9	6
18	12
27	18
36	24
45	30
54	36
	42
	48
	54

6
9 54

6 8
$8\overline{)48}$ $6\overline{)48}$

8	6
16	12
24	18
32	24
40	30
48	36
	42
	48

6
8 48

6 7
$7\overline{)42}$ $6\overline{)42}$

7	6
14	12
21	18
28	24
35	30
42	36
	42

6
7 42

Division Strategy Cards

$7 \overline{)56}$

$56 \div 7$

$7 \overline{)63}$

$63 \div 7$

$8 \overline{)56}$

$56 \div 8$

$9 \overline{)63}$

$63 \div 9$

$8 \overline{)64}$

$64 \div 8$

$8 \overline{)72}$

$72 \div 8$

$9 \overline{)72}$

$72 \div 9$

$9 \overline{)81}$

$81 \div 9$

Card 1

$$9\overline{)63} \quad 7\overline{)63}$$

9	7
18	14
27	21
36	28
45	35
54	42
63	49
	56
	63

7

9 [63]

Card 2

$$8\overline{)56} \quad 7\overline{)56}$$

8	7
16	14
24	21
32	28
40	35
48	42
56	49
	56

7

8 [56]

Card 3

$$7\overline{)63} \quad 9\overline{)63}$$

7	9
14	18
21	27
28	36
35	45
42	54
49	63
56	
63	

9

7 [63]

Card 4

$$7\overline{)56} \quad 8\overline{)56}$$

7	8
14	16
21	24
28	32
35	40
42	48
49	56
56	

8

7 [56]

Card 5

$$9\overline{)81}$$

9
18
27
36
45
54
63
72
81

9

9 [81]

Card 6

$$9\overline{)72} \quad 8\overline{)72}$$

9	8
18	16
27	24
36	32
45	40
54	48
63	56
72	64
	72

8

9 [72]

Card 7

$$8\overline{)72} \quad 9\overline{)72}$$

8	9
16	18
24	27
32	36
40	45
48	54
56	63
64	72
72	

9

8 [72]

Card 8

$$8\overline{)64}$$

8
16
24
32
40
48
56
64

8

8 [64]

Division Strategy Cards

►Find the Area

The area of a rectangle is the number of square units that fit inside of it.

Write a multiplication equation to represent the area of each rectangle.

1.

_____

2.

_____

3.

_____

Make a rectangle drawing to represent each problem. Then give the product.

4. $5 \times 3 = $ _____

5. $7 * 2 = $ _____

6. $2 \cdot 9 = $ _____

Class Activity

Name _____ **Date** _____

▶ Different Ways to Find Area

The large rectangle has been divided into two small rectangles. You can find the area of the large rectangle in two ways:

- Add the areas of the two small rectangles:
  $5 \times 3 =$ ___15___ square units
  $2 \times 3 =$ ___6___ square units
  ___21___ square units

- Multiply the number of rows in the large rectangle by the number of square units in each row:
  $7 \times 3 =$ ___21___ square units

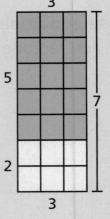

Complete.

7. Find the area of the large rectangle by finding the areas of the two small rectangles and adding them.

   _____

   _____

8. Find the area of the large rectangle by multiplying the number of rows by the number of square units in each row.

   _____

   _____

9. Find this product: $5 \times 4 =$ _____

10. Find this product: $2 \times 4 =$ _____

11. Use your answers to exercises 9 and 10 to find this product: $7 \times 4 =$ _____

　　　　　　　　　　Multiplication and Area

▶ Sprints for 9s

As your teacher reads each multiplication or division, write your answer in the space provided.

× 9	÷ 9
a. _____	a. _____
b. _____	b. _____
c. _____	c. _____
d. _____	d. _____
e. _____	e. _____
f. _____	f. _____
g. _____	g. _____
h. _____	h. _____
i. _____	i. _____
j. _____	j. _____

▶ Identify Types of Problems

Read each problem and decide what type of problem it is. Write the letter from the list below. Then write an equation to solve the problem.

a. Array Multiplication

b. Array Division

c. Repeated Groups Multiplication

d. Repeated Groups Division with an Unknown Group Size

e. Repeated Groups Division with an Unknown Multiplier (number of groups)

f. None of the above

1. Mrs. Ostrega has 3 children. She wants to buy 5 juice boxes for each child. How many juice boxes does she need?

_____

2. Sophie picked 15 peaches from one tree and 3 peaches from another. How many peaches did she pick in all?

_____

3. Zamir brought 21 treats to the dog park. He divided the treats equally among the 7 dogs that were there. How many treats did each dog get?

_____

4. Art said he could make 12 muffins in his muffin pan. The pan has space for 3 muffins in a row. How many rows does the muffin pan have?

_____

5. Bia is helping with the lights for the school play. Each box of light bulbs has 6 rows, with 3 bulbs in each row. How many light bulbs are in each box?

_____

6. Tryouts were held to find triplets to act in a commercial for Triple-Crunch Peanut Butter. If 24 children tried out for the commercial, how many sets of triplets tried out?

_____

Name _____

Date _____

Going Further

► Multiply Using Patterns

Use mental math and patterns to complete.

1. $3 \times 4 =$ _____
    $3 \times 40 =$ _____

2. $10 \times 2 =$ _____
    $100 \times 2 =$ _____

3. $9 \times 8 =$ _____
    $9 \times 80 =$ _____

4. $2 \times 9 =$ _____
    $2 \times 90 =$ _____
    $2 \times 900 =$ _____

5. $5 \times 5 =$ _____
    $5 \times 50 =$ _____
    $5 \times 500 =$ _____

6. $3 \times 4 =$ _____
    $3 \times 40 =$ _____
    $3 \times 400 =$ _____

7. $1 \times 1 =$ _____
    $10 \times 1 =$ _____
    $100 \times 1 =$ _____

8. $2 \times 3 =$ _____
    $20 \times 3 =$ _____
    $200 \times 30 =$ _____

9. $5 \times 6 =$ _____
    $5 \times 60 =$ _____
    $5 \times 600 =$ _____

10. $2 \times 4 =$ _____
    $2 \times 40 =$ _____
    $2 \times 400 =$ _____

11. $5 \times 3 =$ _____
    $5 \times 30 =$ _____
    $5 \times 300 =$ _____

12. $9 \times 2 =$ _____
    $9 \times 20 =$ _____
    $9 \times 200 =$ _____

13. $2 \times 30 =$ _____

14. $5 \times 40 =$ _____

15. $9 \times 60 =$ _____

16. $3 \times 80 =$ _____

17. $2 \times 70 =$ _____

18. $5 \times 90 =$ _____

19. $9 \times 500 =$ _____

20. $5 \times 200 =$ _____

21. $3 \times 300 =$ _____

22. $5 \times 800 =$ _____

23. $9 \times 900 =$ _____

24. $5 \times 600 =$ _____

➡ 25. **On the Back** Describe a pattern you can use to find
    4×200.

Solve and Create Word Problems **249**

Solve and Create Word Problems

▶ Check Sheet 4: 3s and 4s

3s Multiplications	3s Divisions	4s Multiplications	4s Divisions
$8 \times 3 = 24$	$9 / 3 = 3$	$1 \times 4 = 4$	$40 / 4 = 10$
$3 \cdot 2 = 6$	$21 \div 3 = 7$	$4 \cdot 5 = 20$	$12 \div 4 = 3$
$3 * 5 = 15$	$27 / 3 = 9$	$8 * 4 = 32$	$24 / 4 = 6$
$10 \times 3 = 30$	$3 \div 3 = 1$	$3 \times 4 = 12$	$8 \div 4 = 2$
$3 \cdot 3 = 9$	$18 / 3 = 6$	$4 \cdot 6 = 24$	$4 / 4 = 1$
$3 * 6 = 18$	$12 \div 3 = 4$	$4 * 9 = 36$	$28 \div 4 = 7$
$7 \times 3 = 21$	$30 / 3 = 10$	$10 \times 4 = 40$	$32 / 4 = 8$
$3 \cdot 9 = 27$	$6 \div 3 = 2$	$4 \cdot 7 = 28$	$16 \div 4 = 4$
$4 * 3 = 12$	$24 / 3 = 8$	$4 * 4 = 16$	$36 / 4 = 9$
$3 \times 1 = 3$	$15 / 3 = 5$	$2 \times 4 = 8$	$20 / 4 = 5$
$3 \cdot 4 = 12$	$21 \div 3 = 7$	$4 \cdot 3 = 12$	$4 \div 4 = 1$
$3 * 3 = 9$	$3 / 3 = 1$	$4 * 2 = 8$	$32 / 4 = 8$
$3 \times 10 = 30$	$9 \div 3 = 3$	$9 \times 4 = 36$	$8 \div 4 = 2$
$2 \cdot 3 = 6$	$27 / 3 = 9$	$1 \cdot 4 = 4$	$16 / 4 = 4$
$3 * 7 = 21$	$30 \div 3 = 10$	$4 * 6 = 24$	$36 \div 4 = 9$
$6 \times 3 = 18$	$18 / 3 = 6$	$5 \times 4 = 20$	$12 / 4 = 3$
$5 \cdot 3 = 15$	$6 \div 3 = 2$	$4 \cdot 4 = 16$	$40 \div 4 = 10$
$3 * 8 = 24$	$15 \div 3 = 5$	$7 * 4 = 28$	$20 \div 4 = 5$
$9 \times 3 = 27$	$12 / 3 = 4$	$8 \times 4 = 32$	$24 / 4 = 6$
$2 \cdot 3 = 6$	$24 \div 3 = 8$	$10 \cdot 4 = 40$	$28 \div 4 = 7$

Check Sheet 4: 3s and 4s

Name _____ **Date** _____

▶Explore Patterns with 4s

What patterns do you see below?

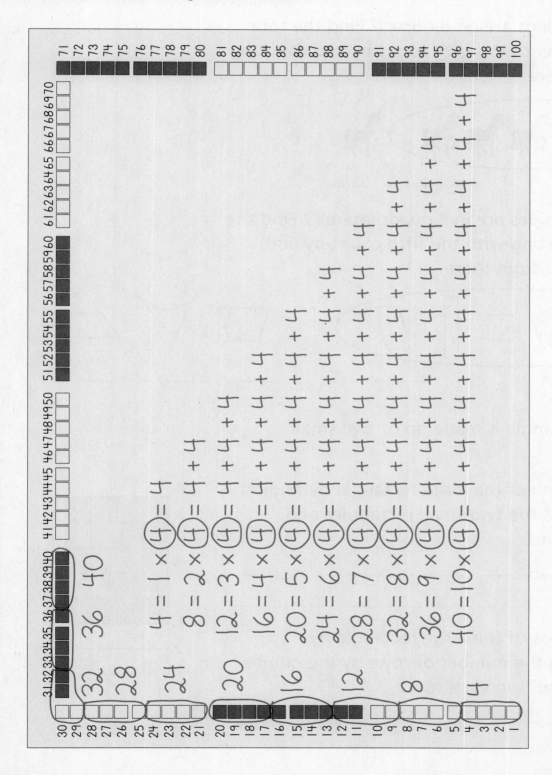

▶ Use the 5s Shortcut for 4s

Solve each problem.

1. How many legs are on 6 horses? Find the total
   by starting with the fifth count-by and counting
   up from there.

_____ _____

2. How many sides are in 8 quadrilaterals? Find the
   total by starting with the fifth count-by and
   counting up from there.

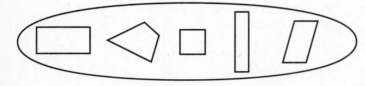   

_____ _____   _____

This large rectangle is made up of two small
rectangles.

3. Find the area of the large rectangle by finding
   the areas of the two small rectangles and
   adding them.

   _____

   _____

4. Find the area of the large rectangle by
   multiplying the number of rows by the number
   of square units in each row.

   _____

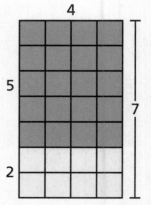

►Use Multiplications You Know

You can combine multiplications to find other multiplications.

This Equal-Shares Drawing shows that 7 groups of 4 is the same as 5 groups of 4 plus 2 groups of 4.

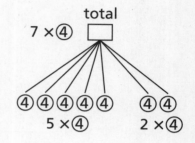

5. Find 5 ×④ and 2 ×④ and add the answers.

_____

6. Find 7 ×④. Did you get the same answer as in exercise 5?

_____

7. Find this product: $5 \times 4 =$ _____

8. Find this product: $4 \times 4 =$ _____

9. Use your answers to exercises 7 and 8 to find this product: $9 \times 4 =$ _____.

►The Puzzled Penguin

Dear Math Students:

Today I had to find 8 × 4. I didn't know the answer, but I figured it out by combining two multiplications I did know:

$$5 \times 2 = 10$$
$$3 \times 2 = 6$$
$$\overline{8 \times 4 = 16}$$

Is my answer right? If not, please help me understand why it is wrong.

Thank you,
The Puzzled Penguin

10. **On the Back** Make a drawing to show that your answers to exercises 7–9 are correct.

Multiply and Divide with 4

▶ Sprints for 3s

As your teacher reads each multiplication or division, write your answer in the space provided.

× 3	÷ 3
a. _____	a. _____
b. _____	b. _____
c. _____	c. _____
d. _____	d. _____
e. _____	e. _____
f. _____	f. _____
g. _____	g. _____
h. _____	h. _____
i. _____	i. _____
j. _____	j. _____

Use the Strategy Cards

►Play *Solve the Stack*

Read the rules for playing *Solve the Stack*. Then play the game with your group.

Rules for *Solve the Stack*

Number of players: 2–4
What you will need: 1 set of multiplication and division Strategy Cards

1. Shuffle the cards. Place them exercise side up in the center of the table.

2. Players take turns. On each turn, a player finds the answer to the multiplication or division on the top card and then turns the card over to check the answer.

3. If a player's answer is correct, he or she takes the card. If it is incorrect, the card is placed at the bottom of the stack.

4. Play ends when there are no more cards in the stack. The player with the most cards wins.

Play *Solve the Stack*

▶ Explore Patterns with 1s

What patterns do you see below?

1.

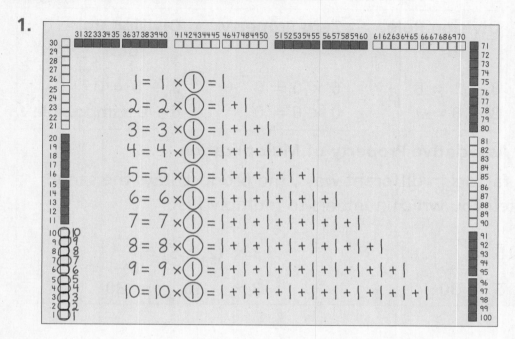

$1 = 1 \times \boxed{1} = 1$

$2 = 2 \times \boxed{1} = 1 + 1$

$3 = 3 \times \boxed{1} = 1 + 1 + 1$

$4 = 4 \times \boxed{1} = 1 + 1 + 1 + 1$

$5 = 5 \times \boxed{1} = 1 + 1 + 1 + 1 + 1$

$6 = 6 \times \boxed{1} = 1 + 1 + 1 + 1 + 1 + 1$

$7 = 7 \times \boxed{1} = 1 + 1 + 1 + 1 + 1 + 1 + 1$

$8 = 8 \times \boxed{1} = 1 + 1 + 1 + 1 + 1 + 1 + 1 + 1$

$9 = 9 \times \boxed{1} = 1 + 1 + 1 + 1 + 1 + 1 + 1 + 1 + 1$

$10 = 10 \times \boxed{1} = 1 + 1 + 1 + 1 + 1 + 1 + 1 + 1 + 1 + 1$

▶ Explore Patterns with 0s

What patterns do you see below?

2.

$1 \times \boxed{0} = 0$

$2 \times \boxed{0} = 0 + 0$

$3 \times \boxed{0} = 0 + 0 + 0$

$4 \times \boxed{0} = 0 + 0 + 0 + 0$

$5 \times \boxed{0} = 0 + 0 + 0 + 0 + 0$

$6 \times \boxed{0} = 0 + 0 + 0 + 0 + 0 + 0$

$7 \times \boxed{0} = 0 + 0 + 0 + 0 + 0 + 0 + 0$

$8 \times \boxed{0} = 0 + 0 + 0 + 0 + 0 + 0 + 0 + 0$

$9 \times \boxed{0} = 0 + 0 + 0 + 0 + 0 + 0 + 0 + 0 + 0$

$10 \times \boxed{0} = 0 + 0 + 0 + 0 + 0 + 0 + 0 + 0 + 0 + 0$

▶ Multiplication Properties and Division Rules

Properties and Rules

Property for 1	Division Rule for 1	Zero Property	Division Rule for 0
$1 \times 6 = 6$ $6 \times 1 = 6$	$8 \div 1 = 8$ $8 \div 8 = 1$	$6 \times 0 = 0$ $0 \times 6 = 0$	$0 \div 6 = 0$ $6 \div 0$ is impossible.

Associative Property of Multiplication

When you group factors in different ways, the product stays the same. The parentheses tell you which numbers to multiply first.

$$(3 \times 2) \times 5 = \boxed{}$$
$$6 \quad \times 5 = 30$$

$$3 \times (2 \times 5) = \boxed{}$$
$$3 \times \quad 10 \quad = 30$$

Find each product.

3. $2 \times (6 \times 1) = \boxed{}$

4. $(4 \times 2) \times 2 = \boxed{}$

5. $7 \times (1 \times 5) = \boxed{}$

6. $(9 \times 8) \times 0 = \boxed{}$

7. $3 \times (2 \times 3) = \boxed{}$

8. $6 \times (0 \times 7) = \boxed{}$

Solve each problem.

Show your work.

9. Shawn gave 1 nickel to each of his sisters. If he gave away 3 nickels, how many sisters does Shawn have? _____

10. Kara has 3 boxes. She put 0 toys in each box. How many toys are in the boxes? _____

11. There are 3 tables in the library. Each table has 2 piles of books on it. If there are 3 books in each pile, how many books are on the tables?

_____

Class Activity

▶Identify Addition and Multiplication Properties

Addition Properties	Multiplication Properties
A. Commutative Property of Addition The order in which numbers are added does not change their sum. $3 + 5 = 5 + 3$	**D. Commutative Property of Multiplication** The order in which numbers are multiplied does not change their product. $3 \times 5 = 5 \times 3$
B. Associative Property of Addition The way in which numbers are grouped does not change their sum. $(3 + 2) + 5 = 3 + (2 + 5)$	**E. Associative Property of Multiplication** The way in which numbers are grouped does not change their product. $(3 \times 2) \times 5 = 3 \times (2 \times 5)$
C. Identity Property of Addition If 0 is added to a number, the sum equals that number. $3 + 0 = 3$	**F. Identity Property of Multiplication** The product of 1 and any number is that number. $3 \times 1 = 3$
	G. Zero Property of Multiplication If 0 is multiplied by a number, the product is 0. $3 \times 0 = 0$

Write the letter of the property that is shown.

12. $1 \times 9 = 9$ _____

13. $5 + (6 + 7) = (5 + 6) + 7$ _____

14. $5 \times 0 = 0$ _____

15. $8 + 0 = 8$ _____

16. $3 \times 9 = \boxed{} \times 3$ _____

17. $(2 \times 1) \times 3 = 2 \times (\boxed{} \times 3)$ _____

▶Use Properties to Solve Equations

Use properties and rules to find the unknown numbers.

18. $5 \times 8 = \boxed{} \times 5$ **19.** $4 + 3 = \boxed{} + 4$ **20.** $0 \div 8 = \boxed{}$

21. $4 \div 4 = \boxed{}$ **22.** $(3 \times 2) \times 4 = 3 \times (\boxed{} \times 4)$ **23.** $6 \times 2 = 2 \times \boxed{}$

24. $5 \times 3 = \boxed{} \times 5$ **25.** $(6 + 2) + 2 = 6 + (\boxed{} + 2)$ **26.** $11 + 0 = \boxed{}$

27. $65 \times 1 = \boxed{}$ **28.** $5 \times (2 \times 6) = (5 \times 2) \times \boxed{}$ **29.** $17 \times 0 = \boxed{}$

▶Use Equations to Demonstrate Properties

Write your own equation that shows the property.

30. Commutative Property of
Multiplication

_____

31. Associative Property of
Addition

_____

32. Identity Property of
Addition

_____

33. Identity Property of
Multiplication

_____

34. Associative Property of
Multiplication

_____

35. Zero Property of
Multiplication

_____

36. Commutative Property of Addition

_____

Class Activity

►**Sprints for 4s**

As your teacher reads each multiplication or division,
write your answer in the space provided.

× 4	÷ 4
a. _____	a. _____
b. _____	b. _____
c. _____	c. _____
d. _____	d. _____
e. _____	e. _____
f. _____	f. _____
g. _____	g. _____
h. _____	h. _____
i. _____	i. _____
j. _____	j. _____

Play Multiplication and Division Games

►Check Sheet 5: 1s and 0s

1s Multiplications	1s Divisions	0s Multiplications
$1 \times 4 = 4$	$10 / 1 = 10$	$4 \times 0 = 0$
$5 \cdot 1 = 5$	$5 \div 1 = 5$	$2 \cdot 0 = 0$
$7 * 1 = 7$	$7 / 1 = 7$	$0 * 8 = 0$
$1 \times 8 = 8$	$9 \div 1 = 9$	$0 \times 5 = 0$
$1 \cdot 6 = 6$	$3 / 1 = 3$	$6 \cdot 0 = 0$
$10 * 1 = 10$	$10 \div 1 = 10$	$0 * 7 = 0$
$1 \times 9 = 9$	$2 / 1 = 2$	$0 \times 2 = 0$
$3 \cdot 1 = 3$	$8 \div 1 = 8$	$0 \cdot 9 = 0$
$1 * 2 = 2$	$6 / 1 = 6$	$10 * 0 = 0$
$1 \times 1 = 1$	$9 / 1 = 9$	$1 \times 0 = 0$
$8 \cdot 1 = 8$	$1 \div 1 = 1$	$0 \cdot 6 = 0$
$1 * 7 = 7$	$5 / 1 = 5$	$9 * 0 = 0$
$1 \times 5 = 5$	$3 \div 1 = 3$	$0 \times 4 = 0$
$6 \cdot 1 = 6$	$4 / 1 = 4$	$3 \cdot 0 = 0$
$1 * 1 = 1$	$2 \div 1 = 2$	$0 * 3 = 0$
$1 \times 10 = 10$	$8 / 1 = 8$	$8 \times 0 = 0$
$9 \cdot 1 = 9$	$4 \div 1 = 4$	$0 \cdot 10 = 0$
$4 * 1 = 4$	$7 \div 1 = 7$	$0 * 1 = 0$
$2 \times 1 = 2$	$1 / 1 = 1$	$5 \times 0 = 0$
$1 \cdot 3 = 3$	$6 \div 1 = 6$	$7 \cdot 0 = 0$

▶ Check Sheet 6: Mixed 3s, 4s, 0s and 1s

3s, 4s, 0s, 1s Multiplications	3s, 4s, 0s, 1s Multiplications	3s, 4s, 1s Divisions	3s, 4s, 1s Divisions
$5 \times 3 = 15$	$0 \times 5 = 0$	$18 / 3 = 6$	$4 / 1 = 4$
$6 \cdot 4 = 24$	$10 \cdot 1 = 10$	$20 \div 4 = 5$	$21 \div 3 = 7$
$9 * 0 = 0$	$6 * 3 = 18$	$1 / 1 = 1$	$16 / 4 = 4$
$7 \times 1 = 7$	$2 \times 4 = 8$	$21 \div 3 = 7$	$9 \div 1 = 9$
$3 \cdot 3 = 9$	$5 \cdot 0 = 0$	$12 / 4 = 3$	$15 / 3 = 5$
$4 * 7 = 28$	$1 * 2 = 2$	$5 \div 1 = 5$	$8 \div 4 = 2$
$0 \times 10 = 0$	$10 \times 3 = 30$	$15 / 3 = 5$	$5 / 1 = 5$
$1 \cdot 6 = 6$	$5 \cdot 4 = 20$	$24 \div 4 = 6$	$30 \div 3 = 10$
$3 * 4 = 12$	$0 * 8 = 0$	$7 / 1 = 7$	$12 / 4 = 3$
$5 \times 4 = 20$	$9 \times 2 = 18$	$12 / 3 = 4$	$8 / 1 = 8$
$0 \cdot 5 = 0$	$10 \cdot 3 = 30$	$36 \div 4 = 9$	$27 \div 3 = 9$
$9 * 1 = 9$	$9 * 4 = 36$	$6 / 1 = 6$	$40 / 4 = 10$
$2 \times 3 = 6$	$1 \times 0 = 0$	$12 \div 3 = 4$	$4 \div 1 = 4$
$3 \cdot 4 = 12$	$1 \cdot 6 = 6$	$16 / 4 = 4$	$9 / 3 = 3$
$0 * 9 = 0$	$3 * 6 = 18$	$7 \div 1 = 7$	$16 \div 4 = 4$
$1 \times 5 = 5$	$7 \times 4 = 28$	$9 / 3 = 3$	$10 / 1 = 10$
$2 \cdot 3 = 6$	$6 \cdot 0 = 0$	$8 \div 4 = 2$	$9 \div 3 = 3$
$4 * 4 = 16$	$8 * 1 = 8$	$2 \div 1 = 2$	$20 \div 4 = 5$
$9 \times 0 = 0$	$3 \times 9 = 27$	$6 / 3 = 2$	$6 / 1 = 6$
$1 \cdot 1 = 1$	$1 \cdot 4 = 4$	$32 \div 4 = 8$	$24 \div 3 = 8$

Check Sheet 6: Mixed 3s, 4s, 0s and 1s

Class Activity

►Play *Multiplication Three-in-a-Row*

Read the rules for playing *Multiplication Three-in-a-Row*. Then play the game with a partner.

Rules for *Multiplication Three-in-a-Row*

Number of players: 2

What You Will Need: A set of multiplication Strategy Cards, *Three-in-a-Row* Game Grids for each player (see page 271)

1. Each player looks through the cards and writes any nine of the products in the squares of a Game Grid. A player may write the same product more than once.

2. Shuffle the cards and place them exercise side up in the center of the table.

3. Players take turns. On each turn, a player finds the answer to the multiplication on the top card and then turns the card over to check the answer.

4. If the answer is correct, the player looks to see if the product is on the game grid. If it is, the player puts an X through that grid square. If the answer is wrong, or if the product is not on the grid, the player does not mark anything. The player then puts the card problem side up on the bottom of the stack.

5. The first player to mark three squares in a row (horizontally, vertically, or diagonally) wins.

Class Activity

▶ Play *Division Race*

Read the rules for playing *Division Race*. Then play the game with a partner.

Rules for *Division Race*

Number of Players: 2
What You Will Need: a set of division Strategy Cards, the *Division Race* game board (see page 272), a different game piece for each player

1. Shuffle the cards and then place them exercise side up on the table.

2. Both players put their game pieces on "START."

3. Players take turns. On each turn, a player finds the answer to the division on the top card and then turns the card over to check the answer.

4. If the answer is correct, the player moves *forward* that number of spaces. If a player's answer is wrong, the player moves *back* a number of spaces equal to the *correct* answer. Players cannot move back beyond the "START" square. The player puts the card on the bottom of the stack.

5. If a player lands on a space with special instructions, he or she should follow those instructions.

6. The first player to reach "END" wins.

                            Play *Division Race*

Name _____   Date _____

Division Race

Start	Move your partner ahead 2 spaces.			Take another turn.	
End					**Skip a turn.**
Slide back!					**Slide ahead!**
Skip a turn.					
	Take another turn.			Send your partner back 2 spaces.	

Division Race Game Board

►Check Sheet 7: 0s, 1s, 2s, 3s, 4s, 5s, 9s and 10s

0s, 1s, 2s, 3s, 4s, 5s, 9s, 10s **Multiplications**	0s, 1s, 2s, 3s, 4s, 5s, 9s, 10s **Multiplications**	1s, 2s, 3s, 4s, 5s, 9s, 10s **Divisions**	1s, 2s, 3s, 4s, 5s, 9s, 10s **Divisions**
$3 \times 0 = 0$	$0 \times 4 = 0$	$9 / 1 = 9$	$40 / 10 = 4$
$7 \cdot 1 = 7$	$5 \cdot 1 = 5$	$4 \div 2 = 2$	$7 \div 1 = 7$
$2 * 2 = 4$	$6 * 7 = 42$	$9 / 3 = 3$	$16 / 2 = 8$
$1 \times 3 = 3$	$2 \times 3 = 6$	$20 \div 4 = 5$	$18 \div 3 = 6$
$4 \cdot 4 = 16$	$5 \cdot 0 = 0$	$15 / 5 = 3$	$16 / 4 = 4$
$6 * 5 = 30$	$1 * 1 = 1$	$45 \div 9 = 5$	$50 \div 5 = 10$
$5 \times 9 = 45$	$10 \times 2 = 20$	$50 / 10 = 5$	$81 / 9 = 9$
$0 \cdot 10 = 0$	$5 \cdot 3 = 15$	$10 \div 1 = 10$	$30 \div 10 = 3$
$0 * 4 = 0$	$4 * 5 = 20$	$8 / 2 = 4$	$10 / 1 = 10$
$1 \times 8 = 8$	$5 \times 6 = 30$	$12 / 3 = 4$	$8 / 2 = 4$
$2 \cdot 5 = 10$	$9 \cdot 7 = 63$	$16 \div 4 = 4$	$27 \div 3 = 9$
$3 * 2 = 6$	$4 * 10 = 40$	$35 / 5 = 7$	$36 / 4 = 9$
$4 \times 3 = 12$	$6 \times 0 = 0$	$27 \div 9 = 3$	$30 \div 5 = 6$
$5 \cdot 4 = 20$	$1 \cdot 6 = 6$	$60 / 10 = 6$	$9 / 9 = 1$
$9 * 6 = 54$	$3 * 2 = 6$	$7 \div 1 = 7$	$80 \div 10 = 8$
$10 \times 7 = 70$	$7 \times 3 = 21$	$8 / 2 = 4$	$10 / 1 = 10$
$0 \cdot 8 = 0$	$4 \cdot 0 = 0$	$18 \div 3 = 6$	$4 \div 2 = 2$
$4 * 9 = 36$	$9 * 5 = 40$	$12 \div 4 = 3$	$21 \div 3 = 7$
$2 \times 0 = 0$	$4 \times 9 = 36$	$40 / 5 = 8$	$8 / 4 = 2$
$1 \cdot 3 = 3$	$10 \cdot 5 = 50$	$36 \div 9 = 4$	$25 \div 5 = 5$

Check Sheet 7: 0s, 1s, 2s, 3s, 4s, 5s, 9s, and 10s

► **Dashes 1–4**

Complete each Dash. Check your answers on page 277.

Dash 1 2s, 5s, 9s, 10s Multiplications	Dash 2 2s, 5s, 9s, 10s Divisions	Dash 3 3s, 4s, 0s, 1s Multiplications	Dash 4 3s, 4s, 1s Divisions
a. $4 \times 5 =$ ___	a. $8 / 2 =$ ___	a. $3 \times 0 =$ ___	a. $12 / 4 =$ ___
b. $10 \cdot 3 =$ ___	b. $50 \div 10 =$ ___	b. $4 \cdot 6 =$ ___	b. $5 \div 1 =$ ___
c. $8 * 9 =$ ___	c. $15 / 5 =$ ___	c. $9 * 1 =$ ___	c. $21 / 3 =$ ___
d. $6 \times 2 =$ ___	d. $63 \div 9 =$ ___	d. $3 \times 3 =$ ___	d. $1 \div 1 =$ ___
e. $5 \cdot 7 =$ ___	e. $90 / 10 =$ ___	e. $8 \cdot 4 =$ ___	e. $16 / 4 =$ ___
f. $10 * 5 =$ ___	f. $90 \div 9 =$ ___	f. $0 * 5 =$ ___	f. $9 \div 3 =$ ___
g. $8 \times 2 =$ ___	g. $35 / 5 =$ ___	g. $1 \times 6 =$ ___	g. $32 / 4 =$ ___
h. $6 \cdot 10 =$ ___	h. $14 \div 2 =$ ___	h. $4 \cdot 3 =$ ___	h. $8 \div 1 =$ ___
i. $9 * 3 =$ ___	i. $27 / 9 =$ ___	i. $7 * 4 =$ ___	i. $24 / 4 =$ ___
j. $2 \times 9 =$ ___	j. $45 / 5 =$ ___	j. $3 \times 7 =$ ___	j. $18 / 3 =$ ___
k. $5 \cdot 8 =$ ___	k. $10 \div 10 =$ ___	k. $0 \cdot 1 =$ ___	k. $10 \div 1 =$ ___
l. $10 * 7 =$ ___	l. $25 / 5 =$ ___	l. $10 * 1 =$ ___	l. $40 / 4 =$ ___
m. $5 \times 5 =$ ___	m. $54 \div 9 =$ ___	m. $4 \times 4 =$ ___	m. $12 \div 3 =$ ___
n. $1 \cdot 5 =$ ___	n. $6 / 2 =$ ___	n. $9 \cdot 3 =$ ___	n. $6 / 3 =$ ___
o. $9 * 6 =$ ___	o. $72 \div 9 =$ ___	o. $8 * 0 =$ ___	o. $4 \div 4 =$ ___
p. $10 \times 10 =$ ___	p. $40 / 5 =$ ___	p. $5 \times 4 =$ ___	p. $7 / 1 =$ ___
q. $4 \cdot 2 =$ ___	q. $80 \div 10 =$ ___	q. $1 \cdot 6 =$ ___	q. $28 \div 4 =$ ___
r. $10 * 8 =$ ___	r. $18 \div 2 =$ ___	r. $3 * 8 =$ ___	r. $24 \div 3 =$ ___
s. $3 \times 9 =$ ___	s. $36 / 9 =$ ___	s. $4 \times 9 =$ ___	s. $20 / 4 =$ ___
t. $9 \cdot 9 =$ ___	t. $30 \div 5 =$ ___	t. $0 \cdot 4 =$ ___	t. $27 \div 3 =$ ___

▶Dashes 1–4

Complete each Dash. Check your answers on page 277.

Dash 1 2s, 5s, 9s, 10s Multiplications	Dash 2 2s, 5s, 9s, 10s Divisions	Dash 3 3s, 4s, 0s, 1s Multiplications	Dash 4 3s, 4s, 1s Divisions
a. $4 \times 5 =$ ___	a. $8 / 2 =$ ___	a. $3 \times 0 =$ ___	a. $12 / 4 =$ ___
b. $10 \cdot 3 =$ ___	b. $50 \div 10 =$ ___	b. $4 \cdot 6 =$ ___	b. $5 \div 1 =$ ___
c. $8 * 9 =$ ___	c. $15 / 5 =$ ___	c. $9 * 1 =$ ___	c. $21 / 3 =$ ___
d. $6 \times 2 =$ ___	d. $63 \div 9 =$ ___	d. $3 \times 3 =$ ___	d. $1 \div 1 =$ ___
e. $5 \cdot 7 =$ ___	e. $90 / 10 =$ ___	e. $8 \cdot 4 =$ ___	e. $16 / 4 =$ ___
f. $10 * 5 =$ ___	f. $90 \div 9 =$ ___	f. $0 * 5 =$ ___	f. $9 \div 3 =$ ___
g. $8 \times 2 =$ ___	g. $35 / 5 =$ ___	g. $1 \times 6 =$ ___	g. $32 / 4 =$ ___
h. $6 \cdot 10 =$ ___	h. $14 \div 2 =$ ___	h. $4 \cdot 3 =$ ___	h. $8 \div 1 =$ ___
i. $9 * 3 =$ ___	i. $27 / 9 =$ ___	i. $7 * 4 =$ ___	i. $24 / 4 =$ ___
j. $2 \times 9 =$ ___	j. $45 / 5 =$ ___	j. $3 \times 7 =$ ___	j. $18 / 3 =$ ___
k. $5 \cdot 8 =$ ___	k. $10 \div 10 =$ ___	k. $0 \cdot 1 =$ ___	k. $10 \div 1 =$ ___
l. $10 * 7 =$ ___	l. $25 / 5 =$ ___	l. $10 * 1 =$ ___	l. $40 / 4 =$ ___
m. $5 \times 5 =$ ___	m. $54 \div 9 =$ ___	m. $4 \times 4 =$ ___	m. $12 \div 3 =$ ___
n. $1 \cdot 5 =$ ___	n. $6 / 2 =$ ___	n. $9 \cdot 3 =$ ___	n. $6 / 3 =$ ___
o. $9 * 6 =$ ___	o. $72 \div 9 =$ ___	o. $8 * 0 =$ ___	o. $4 \div 4 =$ ___
p. $10 \times 10 =$ ___	p. $40 / 5 =$ ___	p. $5 \times 4 =$ ___	p. $7 / 1 =$ ___
q. $4 \cdot 2 =$ ___	q. $80 \div 10 =$ ___	q. $1 \cdot 6 =$ ___	q. $28 \div 4 =$ ___
r. $10 * 8 =$ ___	r. $18 \div 2 =$ ___	r. $3 * 8 =$ ___	r. $24 \div 3 =$ ___
s. $3 \times 9 =$ ___	s. $36 / 9 =$ ___	s. $4 \times 9 =$ ___	s. $20 / 4 =$ ___
t. $9 \cdot 9 =$ ___	t. $30 \div 5 =$ ___	t. $0 \cdot 4 =$ ___	t. $27 \div 3 =$ ___

▶ Answers to Dashes 1–4

Use this sheet to check your answers to the Dashes on page 275.

Dash 1 2s, 5s, 9s, 10s Multiplications	Dash 2 2s, 5s, 9s, 10s Divisions	Dash 3 3s, 4s, 0s, 1s Multiplications	Dash 4 3s, 4s, 1s Divisions
a. $4 \times 5 = 20$	a. $8 / 2 = 4$	a. $3 \times 0 = 0$	a. $12 / 4 = 3$
b. $10 \cdot 3 = 30$	b. $50 \div 10 = 5$	b. $4 \cdot 6 = 24$	b. $5 \div 1 = 5$
c. $8 * 9 = 72$	c. $15 / 5 = 3$	c. $9 * 1 = 9$	c. $21 / 3 = 7$
d. $6 \times 2 = 12$	d. $63 \div 9 = 7$	d. $3 \times 3 = 9$	d. $1 \div 1 = 1$
e. $5 \cdot 7 = 35$	e. $90 / 10 = 9$	e. $8 \cdot 4 = 32$	e. $16 / 4 = 4$
f. $10 * 5 = 50$	f. $90 \div 9 = 10$	f. $0 * 5 = 0$	f. $9 \div 3 = 3$
g. $8 \times 2 = 16$	g. $35 / 5 = 7$	g. $1 \times 6 = 6$	g. $32 / 4 = 8$
h. $6 \cdot 10 = 60$	h. $14 \div 2 = 7$	h. $4 \cdot 3 = 12$	h. $8 \div 1 = 8$
i. $9 * 3 = 27$	i. $27 / 9 = 3$	i. $7 * 4 = 28$	i. $24 / 4 = 6$
j. $2 \times 9 = 18$	j. $45 / 5 = 9$	j. $3 \times 7 = 21$	j. $18 / 3 = 6$
k. $5 \cdot 8 = 40$	k. $10 \div 10 = 1$	k. $0 \cdot 1 = 0$	k. $10 \div 1 = 10$
l. $10 * 7 = 70$	l. $25 / 5 = 5$	l. $10 * 1 = 10$	l. $40 / 4 = 10$
m. $5 \times 5 = 25$	m. $54 \div 9 = 6$	m. $4 \times 4 = 16$	m. $12 \div 3 = 4$
n. $1 \cdot 5 = 5$	n. $6 / 2 = 3$	n. $9 \cdot 3 = 27$	n. $6 / 3 = 2$
o. $9 * 6 = 54$	o. $72 \div 9 = 8$	o. $8 * 0 = 0$	o. $4 \div 4 = 1$
p. $10 \times 10 = 100$	p. $40 / 5 = 8$	p. $5 \times 4 = 20$	p. $7 / 1 = 7$
q. $4 \cdot 2 = 8$	q. $80 \div 10 = 8$	q. $1 \cdot 6 = 6$	q. $28 \div 4 = 7$
r. $10 * 8 = 80$	r. $18 \div 2 = 9$	r. $3 * 8 = 24$	r. $24 \div 3 = 8$
s. $3 \times 9 = 27$	s. $36 / 9 = 4$	s. $4 \times 9 = 36$	s. $20 / 4 = 5$
t. $9 \cdot 9 = 81$	t. $30 \div 5 = 6$	t. $0 \cdot 4 = 0$	t. $27 \div 3 = 9$

Answers to Dashes 1–4

▶ Solve Word Problems with 2s, 3s, 4s, 5s, 6s, 7s, and 9s

Solve each problem.

1. Toni counted 36 legs in the lion house at the zoo. How many lions were there?

_____

2. One wall of an art gallery has a row of 5 paintings and a row of 9 paintings. How many paintings are on the wall?

_____

3. Josh's muffin pan is an array with 4 rows and 6 columns. How many muffins can Josh make in the pan?

_____

4. To get ready for the school spelling bee, Tanya studied 3 hours each night for an entire week. How many hours did she study?

_____

5. The 14 trumpet players in the marching band lined up in 2 equal rows. How many trumpet players were in each row?

_____

6. The Sunnyside Riding Stable has 9 horses. The owners are going to buy new horseshoes for all the horses. How many horseshoes are needed?

_____

Going Further

► Use Patterns to Divide 2- and 3-Digit Numbers

Find each quotient.

1. $8 \div 2 = 8$ ones $\div 2 = 4$ ones or _____

    $80 \div 2 = 8$ tens $\div 2 = 4$ tens or _____

    $800 \div 2 = 8$ hundreds $\div 2 = 4$ hundreds or _____

2. $9 \div 3 = 9$ ones $\div 3 =$ _____ ones or _____

    $90 \div 3 = 9$ tens $\div 3 =$ _____ tens or _____

    $900 \div 3 = 9$ hundreds $\div 3 =$ _____ hundreds or _____

3. $8 \div 4 =$ _____

    $80 \div 4 =$ _____

    $800 \div 4 =$ _____

4. $6 \div 2 =$ _____

    $60 \div 2 =$ _____

    $600 \div 2 =$ _____

5. $6 \div 3 =$ _____

    $60 \div 3 =$ _____

    $600 \div 3 =$ _____

6. $4 \div 2 =$ _____

    $40 \div 2 =$ _____

    $400 \div 2 =$ _____

7. $9 \div 3 =$ _____

    $90 \div 3 =$ _____

    $900 \div 3 =$ _____

8. $25 \div 5 =$ _____

    $250 \div 5 =$ _____

    $2,500 \div 5 =$ _____

9. $36 \div 4 =$ _____

    $360 \div 4 =$ _____

    $3,600 \div 4 =$ _____

10. $72 \div 9 =$ _____

    $720 \div 9 =$ _____

    $7,200 \div 9 =$ _____

11. $54 \div 9 =$ _____

    $540 \div 9 =$ _____

    $5,400 \div 9 =$ _____

Practice with 0s, 1s, 2s, 3s, 4s, 5s, 9s, and 10s

► **Math and Science**

Apatosaurus   Triceratops   Stegosaurus

Take a survey. Find out which dinosaur is the favorite.

1. What question will you ask?   **2.** How many people will you ask?

_____   _____

3. Take the survey. Record your results in the tally chart below.

	Tally	**Total**
Apatosaurus		
Triceratops		
Stegosaurus		

4. Which dinosaur is the favorite? How do you know?

_____

_____

_____

5. What is the difference between the number of votes for the most popular dinosaur and the number of votes for the least popular dinosaur?

_____

Class Activity

► Take a Survey

6. What question would you like to ask in a survey?

_____

_____

_____

7. What answer choices will you have in your survey?

_____

_____

_____

8. How many people will you survey?

_____

9. Take the survey. Record your results in the tally chart below.

	Tally	Total

10. Show the results of the survey in a bar graph.
    Use grid paper to make the graph.

11. Make 3 statements about the results of your survey.

_____

_____

_____

Use Mathematical Processes

Multiply or divide.

1. $8 \times 2 = \boxed{}$ **2.** $5 \cdot 7 = \boxed{}$ **3.** $10 \div 1 = \boxed{}$

4. $81 \div 9 = \boxed{}$ **5.** $4 \times 0 = \boxed{}$ **6.** $63 / 9 = \boxed{}$

7. $6 \cdot 4 = \boxed{}$ **8.** $45 / 5 = \boxed{}$ **9.** $9 \times 3 = \boxed{}$

10. $3\overline{)24}$ **11.** $28 \div 4 = \boxed{}$ **12.** $10 * 8 = \boxed{}$

Write a multiplication equation to find the total number.

13. _____

Without counting the oranges, compare the arrays. Write >, <, or = in the ◯. Then write an equation for each array to show your comparison is correct.

14.    ◯

_____   _____

Write a multiplication equation to represent the area of the rectangle.

15. 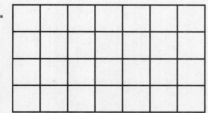   _____

Complete.

16. $9 + 9 + 9 + 9 + 9 + 9 + 9 + 9 =$ _____ $\times \, 9 =$ _____

Write a related division equation.

17. $8 \times 5 = 40$ _____

Write a related multiplication equation.

18. $18 \div 2 = 9$ _____

Write an equation to solve each problem. Then write the answer.

19. Olivia's CD rack has 4 shelves. It holds 8 CDs on a shelf. How many CDs will fit in the rack altogether?

    _____

20. **Extended Response** Paco set up 7 tables to seat 28 children at his birthday party. The same number of children will sit at each table. How many children will sit at each table? Explain how you found your answer. Make a math drawing to help explain.

    _____

    _____

    _____

Glossary

acute angle An angle whose measure is less than 90°.

acute triangle A triangle in which the measure of each angle is less than 90°.

addend A number to be added.

Example: $8 + 4 = 12$

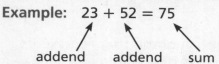

addition A mathematical operation that combines two or more numbers.

Example: $23 + 52 = 75$

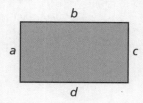

adjacent (sides) Two sides that meet at a point.

Example: Sides a and b are adjacent.

A.M. The time period between midnight and noon.

angle A figure formed by two rays or two line segments that meet at an endpoint.

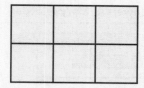

area The number of square units in a region

The area of the rectangle is 6 square units.

array An arrangement of objects, pictures, or numbers in columns and rows.

Associative Property of Addition (Grouping Property of Addition) The property which states that changing the way in which addends are grouped does not change the sum.

Example: $(2 + 3) + 1 = 2 + (3 + 1)$

$$5 + 1 = 2 + 4$$
$$6 = 6$$

Associative Property of Multiplication (Grouping Property of Multiplication) The property which states that changing the way in which factors are grouped does not change the product.

Example: $(2 \times 3) \times 4 = 2 \times (3 \times 4)$

$$6 \times 4 = 2 \times 12$$
$$24 = 24$$

Glossary (Continued)

axis (plural: axes) A reference line for a graph. A bar graph has 2 axes; one is horizontal and the other is vertical.

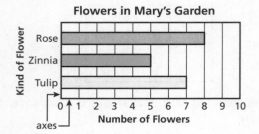

Flowers in Mary's Garden

B

bar graph A graph that uses bars to show data. The bars may be horizontal or vertical.

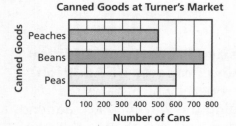

Canned Goods at Turner's Market

base (of a geometric figure) The bottom side of a 2-D figure or the bottom face of a 3-D figure.

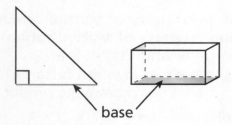

base

C

calculator A tool used to perform mathematical operations.

capacity The amount a container can hold.

cell A rectangle in a table where a column and row meet.

Coin Toss

	Heads	Tails
Sam	11	6
Zoe	9	10

} cell

centimeter (cm) A metric unit used to measure length.

100 cm = 1 m

circle A plane figure that forms a closed path so that all points on the path are the same distance from a point called the center.

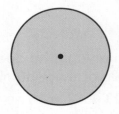

circle graph A graph that represents data as parts of a whole.

Jacket Colors in Ms. Timmer's Class

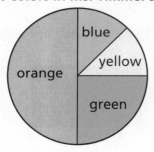

circumference The distance around a circle, about $3\frac{1}{7}$ times the diameter.

column A vertical group of cells in a table.

Coin Toss

	Heads	Tails
Sam	11	6
Zoe	9	10

column

Commutative Property of Addition (Order Property of Addition) The property which states that changing the order of addends does not change the sum.

Example: $3 + 7 = 7 + 3$

$10 = 10$

Commutative Property of Multiplication (Order Property of Multiplication) The property which states that changing the order of factors does not change the product.

Example: $5 \times 4 = 4 \times 5$

$20 = 20$

comparison bars Bars that represent the larger amount, smaller amount, and difference in a comparison problem.

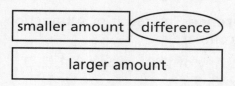

In Volume 2, we use comparison bars for multiplication.

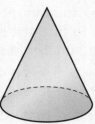

cone A solid figure that has a circular base and comes to a point called the vertex.

congruent figures Figures that have the same size and shape.

Triangles A and B are congruent.

coordinates The numbers in an ordered pair that locate a point on a coordinate grid. The first number is the distance across and the second number is the distance up.

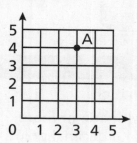

The coordinates 3 and 4 in the ordered pair (3, 4) locate Point *A* on the coordinate grid.

coordinate grid A grid formed by two perpendicular number lines in which every point is assigned an ordered pair of numbers.

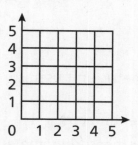

cube A solid figure that has six square faces of equal size.

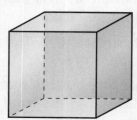

Glossary (Continued)

cup (c) A customary unit of measurement used to measure capacity.

  2 cups = 1 pint
  4 cups = 1 quart
16 cups = 1 gallon

cylinder A solid figure with two congruent circular or elliptical faces and one curved surface.

D

data Pieces of information.

decimal A number with one or more digits to the right of a decimal point.
Examples: 1.23 and 0.3

decimal point The dot that separates the whole number from the decimal part.

    1.23
    ↑
decimal point

decimeter (dm) A metric unit used to measure length

1 decimeter = 10 centimeters

degree (°) A unit for measuring angles or temperature.

degrees Celsius (°C) The metric unit for measuring temperature.

degrees Fahrenheit (°F) The customary unit of temperature.

denominator The bottom number in a fraction that shows the total number of equal parts in the whole.

Example: $\frac{1}{3}$ ← denominator

diagonal A line segment that connects two corners of a figure and is not a side of the figure.

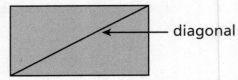
diagonal

diameter A line segment that connects two points on a circle and also passes through the center of the circle. The term is also used to describe the length of such a line segment.

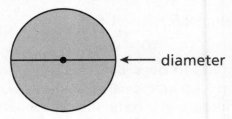
← diameter

difference The result of subtraction or of comparing.

digit Any of the symbols 0, 1, 2, 3, 4, 5, 6, 7, 8, 9.

dividend The number that is divided in division.
Examples:

  $12 \div 3 = 4$ $3\overline{)12}$ = 4

  ↑   ↑
dividend   dividend

division The mathematical operation that separates an amount into smaller equal groups to find the number of groups or the number in each group.
Example: $12 \div 3 = 4$ is a division number sentence.

divisor The number that you divide by in division.
Example: $12 \div 3 = 4$ $3\overline{)12}$ = 4

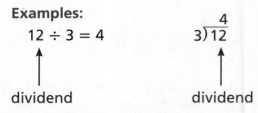
divisor   divisor

E

edge The line segment where two faces of a solid figure meet.

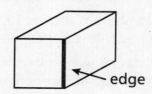

elapsed time The time that passes between the beginning and the end of an activity.

endpoint The point at either end of a line segment or the beginning point of a ray.

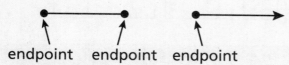

endpoint   endpoint   endpoint

equation A mathematical sentence with an equals sign.

Examples: 11 + 22 = 33
75 − 25 = 50

equilateral triangle A triangle whose sides are all the same length.

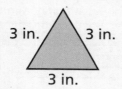

3 in.   3 in.

3 in.

equivalent Equal, or naming the same amount.

equivalent fractions Fractions that name the same amount.

Example: $\frac{1}{2}$ and $\frac{2}{4}$

equivalent fractions

estimate About how many or about how much.

even number A whole number that is a multiple of 2. The ones digit in an even number is 0, 2, 4, 6, or 8.

event In probability, a possible outcome.

expanded form A number written to show the value of each of its digits.

Examples:
347 = 300 + 40 + 7
347 = 3 hundreds + 4 tens + 7 ones

expression A combination of numbers, variables, and/or operation signs. An expression does not have an equals sign.

Examples: 4 + 7 $a - 3$

F

face A flat surface of a solid figure.

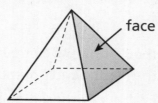

face

factors Numbers that are multiplied to give a product.

Example: 4 × 5 = 20

factor   factor   product

flip To reflect a figure over a line. The size and shape of the figure remain the same.

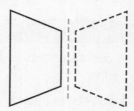

foot (ft) A customary unit used to measure length.

1 foot = 12 inches

Glossary (Continued)

formula An equation with variables that describes a rule.

The formula for the area of a rectangle is:

$A = l \times w$

where A is the area, l is the length, and w is the width.

fraction A number that names part of a whole or part of a set.

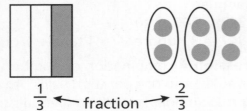

$\dfrac{1}{3}$ ← fraction → $\dfrac{2}{3}$

front-end estimation A method of estimating that keeps the largest place value in a number and drops the rest.

Example: 527 → 500
         + 673 → + 600
         ―――――― 1,100

The 5 in 527 is the "front end" number
The 6 in 673 is the "front end" number

function table A table of ordered pairs that shows a function.

For every input number, there is only one possible output number.

Rule: add 2	
Input	Output
1	3
2	4
3	5
4	6

G

gallon (gal) A customary unit used to measure capacity.

1 gallon = 4 quarts = 8 pints = 16 cups

gram (g) A metric unit of mass, about 1 paper clip.

1,000 grams = 1 kilogram

greater than (>) A symbol used to compare two numbers.

Example: 6 > 5
6 is greater than 5.

group To combine numbers to form new tens, hundreds, thousands, and so on.

growing pattern A number or geometric pattern that increases.

Examples: 2, 4, 6, 8, 10…
1, 2, 5, 10, 17…

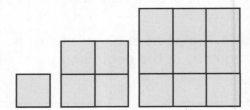

H

height A measurement of vertical length, or how tall something is.

horizontal Extending in two directions, left and right.

horizontal bar graph A bar graph with horizontal bars.

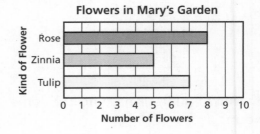

Flowers in Mary's Garden

hundredth One of the equal parts when a whole is divided into 100 equal parts.

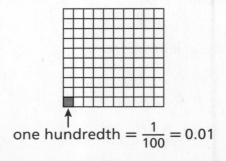

one hundredth = $\dfrac{1}{100}$ = 0.01

I

improper fraction A fraction in which the numerator is equal to or is greater than the denominator. Improper fractions are equal to or greater than 1. $\frac{5}{5}$ and $\frac{8}{3}$ are improper fractions.

inch (in.) A customary unit used to measure length.

12 inches = 1 foot

isosceles triangle A triangle that has at least two sides of the same length.

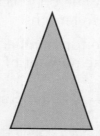

K

key A part of a map, graph, or chart that explains what symbols mean.

kilogram (kg) A metric unit of mass.

1 kilogram = 1,000 grams

kilometer (km) A metric unit of length.

1 kilometer = 1,000 meters

L

less than (<) A symbol used to compare numbers.

Example: 5 < 6
 5 *is less than* 6.

line A straight path that goes on forever in opposite directions.

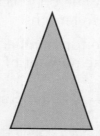

line graph A graph that uses a straight line or a broken line to show changes in data.

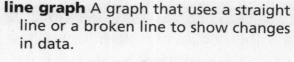

Height of a Bean Plant

line of symmetry A line on which a figure can be folded so that the two halves match exactly.

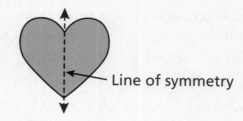

Line of symmetry

line plot A way to show data using a number line.

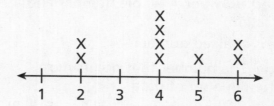

line segment A part of a line. A line segment has two endpoints.

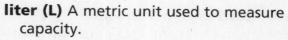

liter (L) A metric unit used to measure capacity.

1 liter = 1,000 milliliters

Glossary (Continued)

M

mass The amount of matter in an object.

mean (average) The sum of the values in a set of data divided by the number of pieces of data in the set.

Example: $3 + 5 + 4 + 8 = 20$
$20 \div 4 = 5$ 5 is the mean

mental math A way to solve problems without using pencil and paper, or a calculator.

meter (m) A metric unit used to measure length.

1 meter = 100 centimeters

method A procedure, or way, of doing something.

mile (mi) A customary unit of length.

1 mile = 5,280 feet

milliliter (mL) A metric unit used to measure capacity.

1,000 milliliters = 1 liter

mixed number A whole number and a fraction.

$1\frac{3}{4}$ is a mixed number.

mode The number that occurs most often in a set of data.

In this set of numbers {3, 4, 5, 5, 5, 7, 8}, 5 is the mode.

multiple A number that is the product of the given number and another number.

multiplication A mathematical operation that combines equal groups.

Example: $4 \times 3 = 12$

factor   factor   product
$3 + 3 + 3 + 3 = 12$
4 times

N

net A flat pattern that can be folded to make a solid figure.

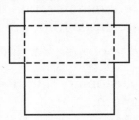

This net can be folded into a rectangular prism.

number line A line on which numbers are assigned to lengths.

numerator The top number in a fraction that shows the number of equal parts counted.

Example: $\frac{1}{3}$ ← numerator

O

obtuse angle An angle that measures more than 90° but less than 180°.

obtuse triangle A triangle with one angle that measures more than 90°.

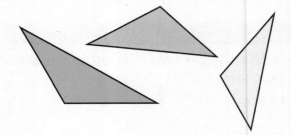

odd number A whole number that is not a multiple of 2. The ones digit in an odd number is 1, 3, 5, 7, or 9.

opposite sides Sides that are across from each other; they do not meet at a point.

Example: Sides *a* and *c* are opposite.

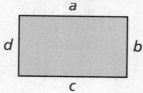

ordered pair A pair of numbers such as (3, 4) in which one number is considered to be first and the other number second. They can name a point on a coordinate grid.

ordinal numbers Numbers used to show order or position.

Example: first, second, fifth

ounce (oz) A customary unit used to measure weight.

16 ounces = 1 pound

parallel lines Two lines that are everywhere the same distance apart.

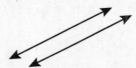

parallelogram A quadrilateral with both pairs of opposite sides parallel.

partner One of two numbers that add to make a total.

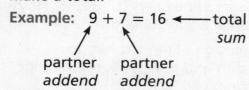

perimeter The distance around the outside of a figure.

perpendicular Two lines or line segments that cross or meet to form right angles.

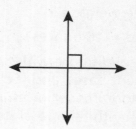

pictograph A graph that uses pictures or symbols to represent data.

pint (pt) A customary unit used to measure capacity.

1 pint = 2 cups

place value The value assigned to the place that a digit occupies in a number.

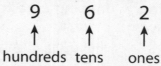

place value drawing A drawing that represents a number. Hundreds are represented by boxes, tens by vertical lines, and ones by small circles.

plane figure A closed figure that has two dimensions.

Glossary (Continued)

P.M. The time period between noon and midnight.

pound (lb) A customary unit used to measure weight.

1 pound = 16 ounces

prism A solid figure with two parallel congruent bases, and rectangles or parallelograms for faces. A prism is named by the shape of its bases.

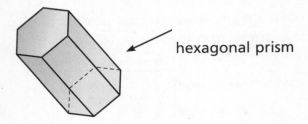

hexagonal prism

probability The chance of an event occurring.

product The answer when you multiply numbers.

Example: $4 \times 7 = 28$

factor   factor   product

proof drawing A drawing used to show that an answer is correct.

$$
\begin{array}{r}
249 \\
+ 386 \\
\underline{11} \\
635
\end{array}
$$

pyramid A solid figure with one base and whose other faces are triangles with a common vertex. A pyramid is named by the shape of its base.

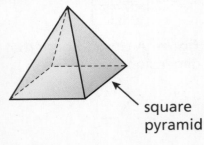

square pyramid

quadrilateral A figure with four sides.

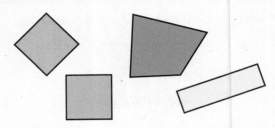

quart (qt) A customary unit used to measure capacity.

1 quart = 4 cups

quotient The answer when you divide numbers.

Examples:

$35 \div 7 = 5$

$7\overline{)35}$ ← quotient

↑ quotient

radius A line segment that connects the center of a circle to any point on the circle. The term is also used to describe the length of such a line segment.

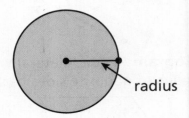

radius

range The difference between the greatest number and the least number in a set of data.

In this set of numbers {12, 15, 18, 19, 20}, the range is 20 − 12 or 8

ray A part of a line that has one endpoint and goes on forever in one direction.

rectangle A parallelogram that has 4 right angles.

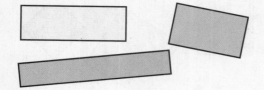

rectangular prism A prism with six rectangular faces.

rectangular pyramid A pyramid with a rectangular base and four triangular faces.

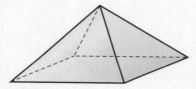

repeating pattern A pattern consisting of a group of numbers, letters, or figures that repeat.

Examples: 1, 2, 1, 2, …

A, B, C, A, B, C, …

rhombus A parallelogram with congruent sides.

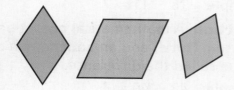

right angle An angle that measures 90°.

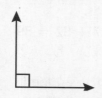

right triangle A triangle with one right angle.

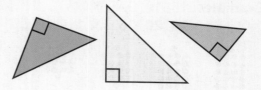

round To find about how many or how much by expressing a number to the nearest ten, hundred, thousand, and so on.

route The path taken to get to a location.

row A horizontal group of cells in a table.

Coin Toss

	Heads	Tails
Sam	11	6
Zoe	9	10

} row

S

scale An arrangement of numbers in order with equal intervals.

scalene triangle A triangle with sides of three different lengths.

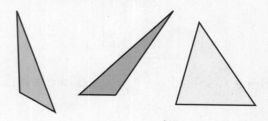

Glossary (Continued)

shrinking pattern A number or geometric pattern that decreases.

Examples: 15, 12, 9, 6, 3,...
25, 20, 16, 13, 11,...

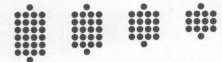

side (of a figure) A line segment that makes up a figure.

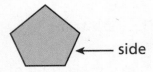

side

simplify To write an equivalent fraction with a smaller numerator and denominator.

slide To move a figure along a line in any direction. The size and shape of the figure remain the same.

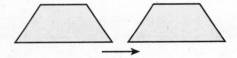

solid figure A figure that has three dimensions.

sphere A solid figure shaped like a ball.

square A rectangle with four sides of the same length.

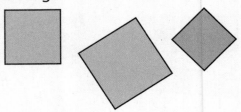

square number A product of a whole number and itself.

Example: $4 \times 4 = 16$

square number

square pyramid A pyramid with a square base and four triangular faces.

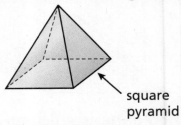

square pyramid

standard form The name of a number written using digits.

Example: 1,829

straight angle An angle that measures 180°.

subtract To find the difference of two numbers.

Example: $18 - 11 = 7$

subtraction A mathematical operation on a sum (total) and an addend, which can be called the difference.

Example: $43 - 40 = 3$

sum The answer when adding two or more addends.

Example: $37 + 52 = 89$

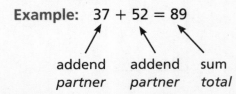

addend addend sum
partner *partner* *total*

survey A method of collecting information.

symmetry A figure has symmetry if it can be folded along a line so that the two halves match exactly.

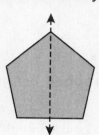

T

table An easy to read arrangement of data, usually in rows and columns.

Coin Toss

	Heads	Tails
Sam	11	6
Zoe	9	10

tally marks Short line segments drawn in groups of 5. Each mark including the slanted marks stands for 1 unit.

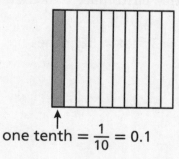 means 13

tenth One of the equal parts when a whole is divided into ten equal parts.

one tenth = $\frac{1}{10}$ = 0.1

thermometer A tool for measuring temperature.

total The answer when adding two or more addends. The sum of two numbers.

Example: 672 + 228 = 900

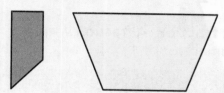

partner *addend* partner *addend* total *sum*

trapezoid A quadrilateral with exactly one pair of parallel sides.

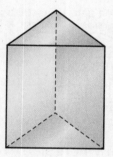

triangular prism A solid figure with two triangular faces and three rectangular faces.

Example:

triangular pyramid A pyramid whose base is a triangle.

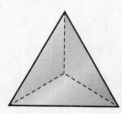

turn To rotate a figure around a point. The size and shape of the figure remains the same.

U

...en up 1 in a given place
...f the next smaller place
...er to subtract.

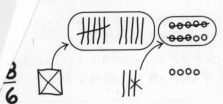

$\dfrac{8}{6}$

...**raction** A fraction with a
...merator of 1.

V

...**enn diagram** A diagram that uses
circles to show the relationship among
sets of objects.

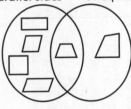

At least one pair of parallel sides   Exactly two sides of equal length

vertex A point where sides, rays, or
edges meet.

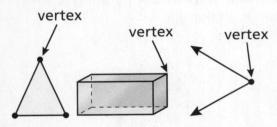

vertex   vertex   vertex

vertical Extending in two directions, up
and down.

vertical bar graph A bar graph with
vertical bars.

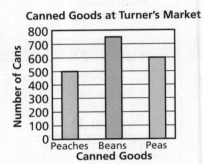

Canned Goods at Turner's Market

W

weight The measure of how heavy
something is.

word form A name of a number written
using words instead of digits.

Example: Nine hundred eighty-four

Y

yard (yd) A customary unit used to
measure length.

1 yard = 3 feet = 36 inches

survey A method of collecting information.

symmetry A figure has symmetry if it can be folded along a line so that the two halves match exactly.

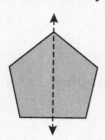

T

table An easy to read arrangement of data, usually in rows and columns.

Coin Toss

	Heads	Tails
Sam	11	6
Zoe	9	10

tally marks Short line segments drawn in groups of 5. Each mark including the slanted marks stands for 1 unit.

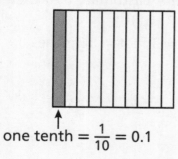 means 13

tenth One of the equal parts when a whole is divided into ten equal parts.

one tenth = $\frac{1}{10}$ = 0.1

thermometer A tool for measuring temperature.

total The answer when adding two or more addends. The sum of two or more numbers.

Example: $672 + 228 = 900$

partner *addend*   partner *addend*   total *sum*

trapezoid A quadrilateral with exactly one pair of parallel sides.

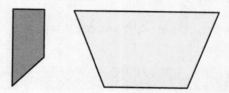

triangular prism A solid figure with two triangular faces and three rectangular faces.

Example:

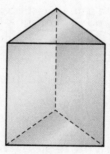

triangular pyramid A pyramid whose base is a triangle.

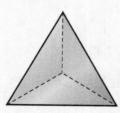

turn To rotate a figure around a point. The size and shape of the figure remains the same.

Glossary (Continued)

ungroup To open up 1 in a given place to make 10 of the next smaller place value in order to subtract.

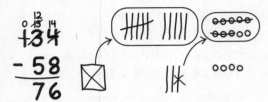

unit fraction A fraction with a numerator of 1.

Venn diagram A diagram that uses circles to show the relationship among sets of objects.

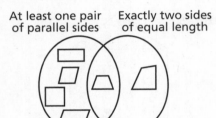

vertex A point where sides, rays, or edges meet.

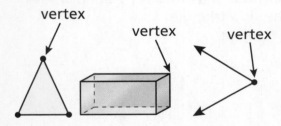

vertical Extending in two directions, up and down.

vertical bar graph A bar graph with vertical bars.

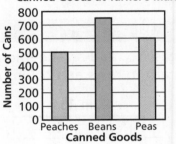

weight The measure of how heavy something is.

word form A name of a number written using words instead of digits.

Example: Nine hundred eighty-four

yard (yd) A customary unit used to measure length.

1 yard = 3 feet = 36 inches